Young Adult Nonfiction

Other Books by the Editors

Teaching Young Adult Literature Today: Insights, Considerations, and Perspectives for the Classroom Teacher

Teaching Young Adults Literature: Integrating, Implementing, and Re-Imagining the Common Core

Young Adult Nonfiction

Gateway to the Common Core

Edited by
Judith A. Hayn, Jeffrey S. Kaplan,
Amanda L. Nolen, and Heather A. Olvey

ROWMAN & LITTLEFIELD
Lanham • Boulder • New York • London

Published by Rowman & Littlefield
A wholly owned subsidiary of The Rowman & Littlefield Publishing Group, Inc.
4501 Forbes Boulevard, Suite 200, Lanham, Maryland 20706
www.rowman.com

Unit A, Whitacre Mews, 26-34 Stannary Street, London SE11 4AB

British Library Cataloguing in Publication Information Available

Library of Congress Cataloging-in-Publication Data

Names: Hayn, Judith A., 1944– editor of compilation. | Kaplan, Jeffrey S., 1951– editor of compilation. | Nolen, Amanda L., editor of compilation. | Olvey, Heather A., editor of compilation.
Title: Young adult nonfiction : gateway to the common core / edited by Judith A. Hayn, Jeffrey S. Kaplan, Amanda L. Nolen, and Heather A. Olvey.
Description: Lanham, Maryland : Rowman & Littlefield, 2015. | Includes bibliographical references and index.
Identifiers: LCCN 2015026466| ISBN 9781475812961 (cloth : alk. paper) | ISBN 9781475812978 (pbk. : alk. paper) | ISBN 9781475812985 (electronic)
Subjects: LCSH: Young adult literature—Study and teaching. | Reading (Elementary) | Reading (Middle school) | Common Core State Standards (Education)
Classification: LCC PN1008.8 .Y685 2015 | DDC 809/.892830712—dc23 LC record available at http://lccn.loc.gov/2015026466

♾™ The paper used in this publication meets the minimum requirements of American National Standard for Information Sciences—Permanence of Paper for Printed Library Materials, ANSI/NISO Z39.48-1992.

Printed in the United States of America

To my sons
Mark Millikan and Brad Hayn

To my husband
Lance Olvey

Contents

Preface

This text grows out of the belief that young adult literature (YAL) has attained a valued place in the English language arts curriculum, and we assert that the genre should have the same status in teaching all aspects of literacy. No matter the location, schools are guided by standards; in many instances these are based on the Common Core State Standards (CCSS). According to the CCSS Initiative website (2015), at the time we are writing, 43 states, the District of Columbia, four territories, and the Department of Defense Education Activity (DoDEA) have adopted the CCSS. One of the principal aspects of the *Common Core State Standards (CCSS) for English Language Arts (ELA) & Literacy in History/Social Studies, Science and Technical Subjects* is the inclusion of specific requirements for the amount of nonfiction versus fiction to be read in grades K–12. Strong (2013) explains that the mandate is designed to do the following:

> The CCSS increase the reading of nonfiction for information in order to (1) build the knowledge and vocabulary of students to enable them to comprehend increasingly complex texts over the grades and (2) help make them more capable of gleaning and writing about information from such texts as they are expected to do in the marketplace and college.

The workforce expects applicants and employees to be adept at comprehending nonfiction, and schools' curricula are even arranged so that textbooks are the main source from which students read. Unfortunately students are oftentimes not taught how to read nonfiction differently across content areas. The lack of instruction in disciplinary literacy is not beneficial to students. Nonfiction YAL can act as a bridge for students to learn how to read in different content areas, can spark interest because it is vastly different from textbooks, and can aid students to delve more deeply into topics, rather than simply gaining surface knowledge.

The intent of this collection of contributions by some of the country's leading literacy experts is to offer practical suggestions for implementing YAL in helping meet the demand that the standards mandate for nonfiction in teaching literacy. The challenges to CCSS abound, but nevertheless, teachers are currently seeking avenues to reach their students no matter what they teach. This text is intended as a primer for those who are dealing with literacy instruction in subject content areas; we advocate YAL as a route. The authors of each chapter validate YAL's ability to do just that and supply a rich selection of texts and strategies.

REFERENCE

Strong, W. H. (2013). *Common Core State Standards: Nonfiction Versus Fiction.* Retrieved from http://www.nas.org/articles/common_core_state_standards_ nonfiction_versus_Fiction.

Introduction

With the Common Core's push to include literacy across content areas, educators need resources to aid them in this endeavor. This book is an effort to do just that. The chapters that discuss ways of using young adult (YA) non-fiction in social studies, science, math, interdisciplinary classes, and science, technology, engineering, and math (STEM) classes in ways that align with the Common Core State Standards (CCSS) are bookended with an introductory chapter on the importance of nonfiction, and a final chapter of annotated resources that can be used. This enables the reader to understand the importance of using young adult literature (YAL) nonfiction before delving into chapters pertaining to different content areas. The annotated resources are at the end of the book, so that by the time the reader has read to that chapter, he or she will be familiar with ways in which they can incorporate the suggested YA texts, as well as find sources for further study.

Hayn and Olvey in chapter 1, "Content Area Literacy and Young Adult Literature: Examining the Possibilities," provide definitions for nonfiction and the immense possibilities that trade books offer for teaching literacy. They suggest strategies and sources for finding YAL that addresses content area knowledge that may more readily attract adolescent readers.

In chapter 2, "An Integrated Curricular Vision: Building Content Knowledge through Textual Connections, Close Reading, and Research Strategies," Wadham discusses the implications of CCSS for those who are not English language arts (ELA) teachers; the standards require that all disciplines include the teaching of literacy. She focuses on social studies and looks at how the inquiry process fits into that content.

Hundley, Bickford, Binford, and Bach continue the focus on social studies in chapter 3, "Range of Reading and Text Complexity: Bringing YA

Historical Fiction to Life with Informational Texts." The authors propose using historical fiction as a bridge to nonfiction texts; they assert that tying history through narrative will develop disciplinary content learning and advance reading and thinking skills. They suggest using fiction that is historically accurate and offer suggestions for determining the primary sources to help students ascertain factual content.

Bull builds on the concept of interdisciplinary teaming of English and science in chapter 4, "Analyzing and Integrating: YA Science Books that Foster Interdisciplinary Connections." She maintains that through content area inquiry and critical thinking, science teachers who collaborate with ELA teachers can promote effective literacy practices across the middle/high school curriculum and provides texts and strategies for accomplishing this. Chapter 5, "Problem Posing and Problem Solving: Using YA Literature to Develop Mathematical Understandings," offers mathematics teachers suggestions for integrating YA nonfiction literature that gives students opportunities to explore key mathematical concepts. Wilkerson, Fetterly, and Wood recommend using nonfiction as a bridge to connect literacy concepts and make sense of moving from narrative to mathematics texts.

Groenke and Prickett in chapter 6 present "Interdisciplinary Opportunities with YA Historical Nonfiction Literature and the Common Core: An Exploration of the Black Freedom Struggle." Beginning with *To Kill a Mockingbird* as a focus text, the authors provide appropriate nonfiction that will enhance the understanding and appreciation of this popular classroom novel. Their chapter is framed through work with preservice English teachers.

Chapter 7, "Graphic Texts as a Catalyst for Content Knowledge and Common Core Content Literacy Standards in STEM Classes," focuses on the technical subjects and the use of graphic informational texts to enhance literacy instruction. Clemmons and Olvey examine the growth of textual resources in the sciences and mathematics and provide activities for teaching three specific nonfiction selections and suggest additional choices.

Finally, chapter 8 offers "Annotated Resources for the Classroom Teacher." Hayn, Layton, and Olvey provide recommendations for professional reading, contemporary YA selections by content area, and websites with suggestions how each might be used to meet the CCSS in literacy. Including literacy standards for science, social studies, and technical subjects intends to complement rather than to replace content standards in those subjects and is indeed the responsibility of teachers in those specific disciplines, making literacy a shared responsibility for all educators.

Chapter 1

Content Area Literacy and Young Adult Literature

Examining the Possibilities

Judith A. Hayn and Heather A. Olvey

> Compared to traditional textbooks, trade books are better able to accommodate the needs of students with diverse backgrounds, interests, needs, and reading levels. They also provide more contextualized, focused, in-depth, and up-to-date coverage of content. They take readers on vicarious journeys that sometimes cannot be readily provided in firsthand classroom explorations.
>
> —Zhihui Fang (2013, p. 274)

THE ABUNDANCE OF NONFICTION

In 1990, Betty Carter and Richard Abrahamson wrote "From magazines to newspapers, cookbooks to textbooks, personal accounts to essays, we are a nation of nonfiction readers (introduction)." That was true then, and remains even more so today with the popularity of the Internet interwoven into adolescents' current culture.

Nonfiction is everywhere we look in our daily lives, but unfortunately many English Language Arts (ELA) teachers are hesitant to teach it because they are not as comfortable with it as they are with teaching fiction (Carter and Abrahamson, 1990; Cole, 2009). For reasons that the authors will investigate, nonfiction is looked down upon as the stepchild of literature (Giblin, 1993), and people assume that nonfiction authors are just compilers of facts without much talent since they only write informational texts (Carter and Abrahamson, 1990; Meltzer, 1994).

The history of nonfiction in the classroom is interesting to explore, and it can tell us much about the direction that educators should take to effectively work it into today's curriculum. There are a myriad of ways to use young adult (YA) nonfiction for the benefit of adolescents, as well as strategies that are effective in teaching this genre. Before delving into these issues it is important to examine how nonfiction is currently viewed in an effort to work past these prejudices and map a new course for current teachers.

TYPES AND VIEWS OF NONFICTION

Today the genre of nonfiction encompasses many things, as well as many terms. The term "informational text" is stigmatized as boring, as well as having an implication that these "informational books [are] on a lower level than their fictional counterparts, and should not aspire to being treated as literature, let alone as works of art" (Giblin, 1993, p. 51). Nonfiction writer Milton Meltzer has much to say to contradict this idea.

Not only does he believe that nonfiction can be literary art based on the simple dictionary definitions of the words literature and art, but he also strives to work past the insulting term. In an interview, Meltzer discusses what the term informational text does to perceptions of readers, and how that affects the writers of this genre. The implication of this particular word is that nonfiction is just an assembly of facts, devoid of emotion. Meltzer maintains that quality nonfiction shows the writer's passion, and "The writer's voice must be heard on the pages of the book" (Carter and Abrahamson, 1990, p. 52).

He argues the art appeal of nonfiction by stating,

> Literary art has, I think, two related aspects: its *subject*, what a book is about, and the *means* the writer uses to convey that material, the *craft*. The craft is the making, shaping, forming, selecting. And what the reader gets from the exercise of the writer's craft upon a subject is an experience. If the subject is significant, and the artist is up to it, then the book can enlarge, it can deepen, it can intensify the reader's experience of life. (Meltzer, 1994, p. 25)

While certainly some nonfiction can be described as informational text, such as some textbooks and reference books, we are fortunate today to have a much wider array of types of nonfiction that allow room for the author's voice, and many of the best come in the form of YA trade books.

Expository text is yet another name for nonfiction, which in its most simple definition means "a text that informs or persuades" (Daniels, 2002, p. 8). To expand upon this idea, students must be taught that there are many different structures that can be used in this type of writing. The confusing thing for students is that oftentimes multiple structures are used within the same text (Daniels, 2002). Teachers must guide students in recognizing the different structures. In addition to helping students navigate expository text, teachers must also acknowledge that expository text is not just informational, but it can also be enjoyable to read (Sullivan, 2001).

The final type of nonfiction that will be discussed is the subgenre known as new journalism, in which the nonfiction novel, editorials, op-ed pieces, and creative nonfiction all fall. This is where the lines between fiction and nonfiction blur (Cole, 2009; Lamb, 2010; Moss, Leone, and Dipillo, 1997), because the author takes known facts and creates dialogues and situations within which the characters interact. The characters are based on real people, but they have fabricated conversations, often in fictionalized ways because the writer has no choice but to take certain liberties to get the story across since the particular conversations and ways in which things happened are lost to history. We know the outcomes of things, not necessarily how things came to be.

Mary Lamb (2010) believes that students need help navigating the field of nonfiction in general, not just when fiction and nonfiction are intentionally combined in one work, because this digital age causes students to "have a tenuous grasp on the differences between fiction and nonfiction, which can result in a lack of critical thinking about important political and cultural issues" (p. 43). Another reason students need help understanding and analyzing nonfiction is the fact that students are inundated with it everywhere except in their ELA classes, which is where it is expected that students will be taught how to read different types of texts.

Unfortunately it is often assumed that students have achieved literacy by the time they reach high school, so time is not spent on improving literacy for students. Textbooks abound in content classes, full of informational text, and "standardized reading tests contain 70–80% expository text" (Daniels, 2002, p. 7). How can we expect students to comprehend what they are reading in other classes, or do well on standardized tests if we do not take time to teach them *how* to read the different forms in this genre? It is known that comprehending nonfiction requires a different skill set than reading narrative text (Antonacci and O'Callaghan, 2011), so teachers should be diligent in sharpening those skills for students.

Why are so many ELA teachers hesitant to teach nonfiction? There are many reasons, some of which include; (1) that it is habit for ELA teachers to teach fiction, (2) there is a romantic view of fiction that promotes the idea that people can only gain insight to humanity through this genre, (3) many teachers don't know how to teach students to read for information, (4) teachers have a lack of exposure to the genre, and (5) there is a longstanding myth that adolescents do not like it (Cole, 2009). All of these hurdles must be overcome in order for nonfiction to take its rightful place in the curriculum.

WHY NONFICTION YOUNG ADULT LITERATURE SHOULD BE TAUGHT IN ALL CONTENT CLASSES

It is known that access to books is critical to get students to read in general, and most avid readers have that access at home (Young and Moss, 2006). For those who do not have that benefit at home, it is the job of school and class-room libraries to supply books, since students read more in classrooms with libraries simply because they have access (Young and Moss, 2006). Before a discussion on how teachers can give their students better access begins, it is important to note why it should be there in the first place. What are the benefits of YA nonfiction trade books?

Studies have lain to rest the myth that teens do not like nonfiction. Glenda Childress' 1984 study showed that 40 percent of the books checked out of her school library during the time she examined circulation records was nonfiction. (Abrahamson and Carter, 1992). George Norvell found that by the fourth grade, students' interest in nonfiction grows, particularly for males, and as children grow into adolescents, so does their appreciation for the genre (Abrahamson and Carter, 1992; Young and Moss, 2006; Young, Moss, and Cornwell, 2007).

A study conducted in Canada in 2003 found that students actually checked out twice as many nonfiction books as they did fiction (Young, Moss, and Cornwell, 2007). In 1992, Abrahamson and Carter monitored circulation records from three junior high school libraries to see not only how much nonfiction was being checked out, but also what types. They noted that the majority of the books they examined were not checked out for assignments; rather, they were for pleasure reading.

The trend they noticed was that the most popular nonfiction books required some kind of involvement from the reader, such as "how to" books, drawing books, and sports books. Even *The Guinness Book of World Records*, which they found to be the most popular nonfiction book in all three of the schools they examined, can require something from the reader. While reading, the adolescent probably thinks about what it would be like to set some of those records, so they are not only collecting facts, but also wondering about the world around them (Abrahamson and Carter, 1992).

If teachers know that teens do, in fact, read nonfiction for entertainment, they can use this fact to their benefit. If teens enjoy it, they will read more, and an "increase in voluntary reading contributes to gains in reading achieve-ment" (Young and Moss, 2006). Furthermore, trade books have an additional enticement; many YA nonfiction texts read like fiction stories with the added benefit of containing original pictures and documents that the author used in research to aid in writing the book.

Other reasons to teach nonfiction include the fact that it gives students a chance to examine a text that has not been overanalyzed (Kirby and Kirby,

2010). The majority of the literature taught in high school has been analyzed so much, that there is little, if anything, new to say about it. Students have the opportunity to form opinions on expository works without fear of "getting it wrong."

Also, by using different medias of nonfiction, such as magazine and newspaper articles, and documentaries, it becomes easier to link teaching to students' lives (Welsh, 2014), thus exposing students to a variety of types of text (Hirth, 2002; Palmer and Stewart, 1997; Young, Moss, and Cornwell, 2007). Showing students various forms of different genres will help students transition into the different types of reading they will do in college and beyond. Adults read a lot of nonfiction in their daily lives, so exposure to it in junior and high school will help prepare students more fully for life after school.

THE BENEFITS OF USING YA TRADE BOOKS

So what are the benefits of YA nonfiction trade books being used across all content areas? There are many, and the authors would be remiss if they did not again state first and foremost, that teens enjoy reading nonfiction; therefore, they become engaged readers, which leads to the desire to read more resulting in greater literacy (Galda and Cullinan, 1991). One reason for this is the difference in the writing styles between textbooks and trade books, but it is also because trade books allow students to hone in on a particular event rather than a series of things that happened, whereas a textbook typically states information in broad and impersonal terms.

This difference in the writing style of trade books connects the reader to the event, and oftentimes allows for an emotional response, while also permitting a certain issue to be examined in depth (Young, Moss, and Cornwell, 2007). For example, with textbooks students learn facts about the Holocaust in general, but with Neal Bascomb's 2014 Young Adult Library Services Association (YALSA) award–winning book *The Nazi Hunters: How a Team of Spies and Survivors Captured the World's Most Notorious Nazi*, teens get a front row seat in the hunt for Adolf Eichmann, who was one of the most sought-after Nazis after the war.

Readers learn not only about the hunt and capture of this man and why he is the most notorious Nazi, but they also delve into the thoughts and feelings of the people who were involved in his arrest, the points of view of Eichmann's family members, and they most certainly finish the book with a more personal connection to the Holocaust than the textbook alone could ever give them.

Nonfiction also introduces students to academic vocabulary, while at the same time exposing them to different text types (Palmer and Stewart, 1997;

Young, Moss, and Cornwell, 2007), which are both important skills required by the Common Core State Standards (CCSS). Students are expected to read and write nonfiction across the content areas, but they don't have much experience deconstructing it. Exposing them to YA nonfiction gives students practice reading the genre (Carter and Abrahamson, 1990; Palmer and Stewart, 1997), while at the same time helping them transition to the more sophisticated reading that is required of them in content area textbooks (Shanahan and Shanahan, 2008).

We live in the Information Age, where people are exposed to information all day every day (Moss, Leone, and Dipillo, 1997). For this reason, there is a growing need for students to be fluently literate across the disciplines because of the change that has taken place in the work place (Shanahan and Shanahan, 2008). Jobs that once did not require literacy, now do, and it is our job as educators to prepare students for this reality.

HOW TO USE YA NONFICTION

So how do we, as teachers, instruct students how to read nonfiction? First, we must use different questioning strategies than the ones currently employed for fiction. It is not as easy as asking students to talk about the character, plot, or theme; different types of questions must be asked. Many authors have cited Carter and Abrahamson's (1990) guiding questions for teachers to use in conjunction with nonfiction (Cole, 2009; Sullivan, 2001); however, they bear repeating here.

1. How would this book be different if it had been written ten years earlier? Ten years later?
2. Which illustrations do you wish you had taken or drawn yourself? Why?
3. Compare this nonfiction book with another one written on the same topic. How do they differ? How are they alike? Which one do you like better (or believe more)? Why?
4. What segment, portion, or focus of this book would make a good documentary? Why?
5. What steps do you think the author followed to research and write this book?
6. How would this book be different if it had been written for a fourth grader?
7. What kind of teacher do you think the author would make?
8. If you had a chance to interview the authors of this book, what would you ask them?

9. Tell me three facts, theories, or incidents that you found particularly interesting. Now, assume you haven't read the book. Can you find this information? Why or why not?
10. Look at the title and the jacket of this book. What do they indicate the book will be about? Do they give a fair representation of the book's contents? (pp. 185–87)

Obviously, not every question will or should work with every nonfiction text; however, this list is an excellent resource with which to begin planning a lesson. Many of these questions prompt students not only to predict what they think about certain aspects of nonfiction, but also to use their critical thinking skills as well as research skills.

For example, number ten asks students to predict what the book will be about based on the cover illustrations, and number one asks readers to examine not only how facts have changed, but also how facts are likely to change in the future, thereby acknowledging that nonfiction texts can become outdated based on what scientists and historians learn. The prediction required in number one also requires students to use their critical thinking skills.

Number six is especially geared toward critical thinking by asking students to determine how a nonfiction text would be different for a younger reader. This requires them to think about what should be left out, added, or done differently based on the author's intended audience, which is in direct correlation with CCSS RI.9–10, 11–12.6: "Determine an author's point of view or purpose in a text and analyze how an author uses rhetoric to advance that point of view or purpose" (2010).

Research skills are analyzed when students are asked to answer question five, which requires a determination of what an author had to do in order to write the text. Students are expected to be able to find sources and synthesize information into coherent writing in high school, so asking this question exposes them to the idea of the research process (Palmer and Stewart, 1997).

In analyzing the author's purpose in writing a particular text, students must be taught that as readers they also have different purposes for reading, particularly when reading nonfiction, and oftentimes those purposes overlap. For example, reading to acquire information is not the only motive for reading nonfiction. People also read this genre to satisfy their own curiosity, to understand the world around them better, to expand vocabulary as well as understand new concepts, to enjoy themselves, and to make a connection between what is being learned and the lives of the readers themselves (Harvey, 1998).

Since students read nonfiction for different purposes, a vital lesson for them is to understand which purpose or purposes for which they are reading, so that they know how to read a certain piece. Reading only to gain information takes a different skill set than reading to enjoy oneself, or to satisfy curiosity. Harvey (1998) makes an analogy that teens can understand well; people read for different purposes just as they watch television for different reasons. One watches *The History Channel* with a different sort of attention than when watching a favorite sitcom. We, as viewers or readers, expect different things from the diverse genres.

In addition to asking different types of questions for nonfiction, and training students to identify the reasons they are reading a particular piece, attention must be devoted to how educators can gain their students' interest in reading nonfiction. Teachers are familiar with many strategies that can be used for fiction and work just as well for nonfiction.

For example, nonfiction is not often used for reading aloud to students, but it has been shown that students view it as a favorable activity (Abrahamson and Carter, 1992). Reader's Theater, which has been used with success with fiction in ELA classes, can also be used successfully with YA nonfiction texts (Young, Moss, and Cornwell, 2007).

Teachers and librarians can both garner students' interest by using YA non-fiction books in displays, as well as for book talks (Carter and Abrahamson, 1990; Young, Moss, and Cornwell, 2007). Literature circles are a fantastic way to use nonfiction trade books in the class, especially when a teacher either needs to have different titles available for either reasons of interest, variety, or to make sure students with varying reading levels have appropriate options (Daniels, 2002).

A critical thing that teachers can do to promote nonfiction of any kind, particularly YA nonfiction, is to make it available in their classroom libraries, but simply having it available is not enough. Teachers must make students aware of the availability by talking about the books, either through book talks, or by mentioning titles of interest to certain students, or even to the class as a whole if it relates to what is being studied. If possible, it is a good idea to have multiple copies of YA nonfiction in the class library so that several students can read it at once (Young, Moss, and Cornwell, 2007), which will hopefully lead to meaningful student-driven conversations about the text.

Having text sets available by topic or theme in the classroom allows students to explore a topic in more depth than a text book allows, as well as supporting "conversations that consider multiple perspectives and invite students to engage in sophisticated synthesis of information" (Coombs, 2013, p. 11). If students are aware through the teacher's instruction that the text sets exist, they know they can easily find a book related to a topic of interest, or something related to what is currently being studied.

Another effective idea is to actually involve the students in the maintenance and organization of the class library (Young, Moss, and Cornwell, 2007).

By examining the books to determine how to organize them, students will find themselves scanning and reading sections of many different books, both familiarizing themselves with what is available, as well as finding certain texts that they want to read completely at a later date.

A different way to familiarize students with YA nonfiction is to employ the use of book passes, or play the game "Guess the Fib" (Young, Moss, and Cornwell, 2007). To facilitate the book pass activity, each student is given a YA nonfiction text with instructions that they have three minutes to review the book and then write what they learned about it on a piece of paper that accompanies the book, known as the book pass. The books and passes are then passed to the next student, and the cycle repeats four to five times.

"Guess the Fib" is executed in groups. The students in each group craft three statements about a YA nonfiction text; two of which are true, and one which is false. The rest of the class attempts to guess which statement is incorrect. This activity can pique students' interest simply by the statements which surprisingly turn out to be true.

WHERE TO FIND QUALITY YA NONFICTION

Once the hurdles of stigma and commonly believed myths, teachers being unfamiliar with teaching nonfiction, and unavailability for students have been overcome, the next logical question becomes, "How do teachers find quality YA nonfiction books?" Where does one begin looking for titles to either review or acquire? A good place to start is the YALSA's award lists. There is a category for nonfiction, and it is awarded annually. In addition to the winner, the finalists are listed, and the lists go back to 2010.

Teachers can also check with their school librarians, which have been shown to be underused resources (Palmer and Stewart, 1997), to see not only what titles are currently in the school library, but also what is available. New titles can often be acquired if a teacher requests it. Reviewing past issues of *Voice of Youth Advocates (voya)* can lead one to many nonfiction titles since each issue reviews several nonfiction YA trade books.

The National Science Teachers Association also creates an annual list of "Outstanding Science Tradebooks for Students K-12" (Fang, 2013, p. 275). There are also specialized websites for different content areas that are helpful as well, such as the American Association for the Advancement of Science (www.aaas.org), NCTE, or the National Council of Teachers of English (www.ncte.org), as well as NCSS, or National Council for the Social Studies (http://www.socialstudies.org/resources/notable).

POSSIBILITIES

So, what are the possibilities that these trade books can offer? It of course depends upon the book, as well as teachers' willingness to move beyond the comfort of textbooks. Once student engagement in topics is evident through the use of YA nonfiction, teachers will, no doubt, realize that the effort to incorporate these books into existing curriculum is well worth it. Let us take a look at some recent titles and examine how they can be used in content area classes. There are not as many titles available for certain subjects, but with a little ingenuity and some research one can find YA nonfiction trade books to fit any class.

The authors' suggestions will begin with one of the subjects that poses a bit more difficulty in finding nonfiction trade books; mathematics. While there are not as many titles available as for, say, Social Studies, there are still options from which to choose. Danica McKellar has written several books aimed at girls, to help with different math concepts, including math in general, prealgebra, and her most recent topic, geometry.

In *Girls Get Curves: Geometry Takes Shape*, McKellar tries to relate geometric concepts to girls' lives to make the ideas more understandable. For example, one of the first concepts she introduces is conditional statements, and she does so by using a common teen problem; a girl's best friend dating a boy she herself has a crush on. By using "if, then" statements, she explains that the situation is different based on what is known. For example, *if* your friend knows that you like said boy, *then* you have a reason to be mad at her, but *if* she does not know you have feelings for him, *then* you are partially to blame since you never told her (McKellar, 2013).

By using every day experiences, McKellar attempts to demystify mathematics concepts. This book, and others by McKellar, would be beneficial to have in classroom libraries, as recommendations by teachers to girls who are struggling with concepts, or even for use in literature circles.

To explore math from a different angle, a book such as *Cathedral: The Story of Its Construction*, by David Macaulay discusses the intricacies of architecture and building. Excerpts of this text could be used to emphasize a real-life application of not only geometrical concepts, but also measuring, and possibly even algebra. This book could be the basis of a project-based learning (PBL) project, by assigning students to read it and then to take what they learned and attempt to design something on a small scale.

There are many titles that lend themselves to the social studies classroom by helping students learn more about certain historical events through storytelling, thus helping students understand a period or concept in history better. In addition to the previously mentioned book by Bascomb, another book dealing with the Holocaust is *Hidden Like Anne Frank: 14 Stories of Survival* by Marcel Prins and Peter Henk Steenhuis.

This book would be a great supplement for a unit on World War II, since the stories are short, and teachers can pick and choose a few stories to use. The brevity of the stories also makes them ideal for small group work. Undoubtedly, even if the entire text is not used in class, students will be interested enough to read more than the assigned chapters.

Another 2014 YALSA award finalist that would also work well in a World-War-II unit is *Courage Has No Color: The True Story of the Triple Nickles.* This book tells the story of America's first black paratroopers who fought during World War II, despite the fact that they, as African Americans, did not have many rights in the country for which they were fighting.

Not only will this book force students to learn about what these soldiers went through in those tumultuous times, but the author also includes a discussion at the end about how she researched for the book. This section, "The Story Behind the Story" would be beneficial to use to help students understand some necessary components for research, thus aiding them in gathering and synthesizing skills.

City of the Dead could be used in either a social studies class, or even a science class since it tells the story of the Galveston Hurricane. A note of caution should be issued with this book, however, because it is in fact one of the books that blends the lines between fact and fiction a bit more than the previously mentioned titles. It is based upon real events, and has actual pictures from the disaster, but the author took a bit of liberty telling the story making this a book that leans more toward historical fiction, but it is still strongly rooted in fact. This distinction would definitely need to be addressed if it is chosen to use as a class text.

If used in a science class, this text could supplement a unit on natural disasters. Reading this book would give students an insider's view of what it is like to be in the middle of a hurricane. Students could be asked to rely on their own experiences, if they have experienced a tornado, hurricane, or even a typhoon, and a project differentiating different natural disasters could ensue.

A science book on an entirely different subject has recently been published, entitled *Women in Space: 23 Stories of First Flights.* Since this is a book of short stories, it could be used as was previously suggested for *Hidden Like Anne Frank*; by choosing a few of the stories to supplement a study on space.

To continue the space theme, *Curiosity's Mission on Mars: Exploring the Red Planet* teaches students not only about exploring Mars, but also about how the space rover Curiosity works and gathers scientific data. The text of this book is only 51 pages, so it would lend itself well to a whole class assigned reading.

It offers students many areas for further study, thus lending itself to research projects that could be completed and presented in small groups. Possible topics include NASA technology that is now used in everyday life, creating a timeline of past space missions, or even asking students to determine what types of problems could occur if our civilization were to terraform another planet.

There are two nonfiction books worthy of mention for use in ELA classes that were not necessarily marketed with a YA audience in mind, but would lend themselves well to this audience. The first is Katherine Howe's *The Penguin Book of Witches*. Being a college professor who sometimes teaches "The Crucible," and having an interest in this period of history, Howe recently wrote a YA fiction book called *Conversion*, which deals with the Salem witch trials.

The Penguin Book of Witches includes the source documents that she used in her research for *Conversion*, thus making an interesting addition to any class that reads "The Crucible." (These three works also happen to be a great start for a text set.) The documents that are the basis for the myriad of fictional pieces about the Salem witch trials make for interesting reading, and can propel students into an investigation of what facts were made up, and why.

The other text is entitled *"Scribbling Women": True Tales From Astonishing Lives.* Marthe Jocelyn tells the stories of eleven women writers who wrote during times and in places where women were not considered capable of writing anything of merit. The title for the book came from a term coined by Nathaniel Hawthorne who complained about "scribbling women," whom he found to be annoying.

Different stories in this book could be assigned to various small groups, with the intention of teaching the entire class about the women and their writings. After hearing about all of the women, students could be assigned the task of writing their own account by imagining that they live in a time in which a certain sex—which one depends upon the sex of the writer—is looked down upon for writing. Students would have to imagine what things in daily life he or she would find interesting enough to write about, making sure to include some reference that the opposite sex is deemed worthy of authorship, while the writer's sex is not.

An interesting book that could be used in either art classes, or even in STEM schools as a technology text, is Chip Kidd's *Go: A Kidd's Guide to Graphic Design*, which also happens to be a finalist for the 2014 YALSA awards. This text is an informative and visually appealing book. Kidd explores topics including typography, image quality, patterns, imagery, and color theory, to name a few. There are even six design project suggestions in the back that teachers could use as is, or as a starting point for a bigger project.

This is a book that definitely includes both aesthetic and efferent reasons for reading (Cole, 2009), because even thumbing through the book is enjoyable, not to mention the amount of important information it contains. This text could be used as required reading when graphic design is being taught since it covers many important concepts, and has such a wonderful use of graphics and color, which will absolutely aid in student engagement. The class could be broken up into small groups, and each group could be required to teach a couple of the chapters to the rest of the class, thus aiding in student ownership of learning.

There are a couple of recent titles worth mentioning for use in health classes. The first, *Words Wound: Delete Cyberbullying and Make Kindness Go Viral* is a guide that deals with the issue of cyberbullying by using facts, surveys, tips, and personal stories. It has something in it for all teens, whether bullies themselves, the target of bullying, or uninvolved bystanders. There is also a leader's guide now available for free download that can help with planning and teaching the book.

This is another text that can be used as a whole class text, and can be broken up into mini-lessons throughout the year. It lends itself to small group work, since this subject allows for more research to extend some of the chapters. Another small group option is to have students create and act out different cyberbullying scenarios with appropriate ways to handle them.

An additional option for health class is a book entitled *Dear Teen Me: Authors Write Letters to Their Teen Selves.* This book deals with the lack of self-esteem many teens have, drug use, sexuality, and even epilepsy. Different letters can be chosen for the various health topics that must be taught, and the great thing is that the overarching message of each letter (and the book as a whole) is that whatever issues teens are dealing with right now, they will ultimately, if they don't give up, survive it; and that's something every teen needs to repeatedly hear.

The authors believe that there is not only a place for nonfiction across all content areas, but also a need. Nonfiction YA books engage students, give them a deeper knowledge on a given topic, expose them to the expository text that they must learn to navigate in school and beyond, and speak to adolescents' desire to learn in a fun way. Today's nonfiction books are visually appealing, informative as well as entertaining, and the use of photographs and personal stories serve to strengthen concepts and ideas for teens. Just as there are a multitude of different YA nonfiction titles available covering a myriad of topics, there are also countless possibilities for the ways in which to use them in content area classes.

Table 1.1   YA Nonfiction Titles

Book Title	Author	Content Class
Cathedral: The Story of Its Construction	David Macaulay	Math
City of the Dead: Galveston Hurricane, 1900	T. Neill Anderson	Science
Courage Has No Color: The True Story of the Triple Nickles	Tanya Lee Stone	Social Studies
Dear Teen Me: Authors Write Letters to Their Teen Selves	Kristin Anderson and Miranda Kenneally	Health
The Freedom Summer Murders	Don Mitchell	Social Studies
Go: A Kidd's Guide to Graphic Design	Chip Kidd	Art, Technology
Girls Get Curves: Geometry Takes Shape	Danica McKellar	Math
Hidden Like Anne Frank: 14 Stories of Survival	Marcel Prins and Peter Henk Steenhuis	Social Studies
The Nazi Hunters: How a Team of Spies and Survivors Captured the World's Most Notorious Nazi	Neal Bascomb	Social Studies
The Penguin Book of Witches	Katherine Howe	English
"Scribbling Women:" True Tales From Astonishing Lives	Marthe Jocelyn	English
Women in Space: 23 Stories of First Flights	Karen Bush Gibson	Science
Words Wound: Delete Cyberbullying and Make Kindness Go Viral	Justin W. Patchin and Sameer Hinduja	Health

REFERENCES

Abrahamson, R. F., and Carter, B. (1992). What we know about nonfiction and young adult readers and what we need to do about it. *Publishing Research Quarterly, 8*(1), 41–54.

Antonacci, P. A., and O'Callaghan, C. M. (2011). *Developing Content Area Literacy: 40 Strategies for Middle and Secondary Classrooms.* Thousand Oaks, CA: Sage.

Bascomb, N. (2013). *The Nazi Hunters: How a Team of Spies and Survivors Captured the World's Most Notorious Nazi.* New York, NY: Arthur A. Levine Books.

Carter, B., and Abrahamson, R. F. (1990). In *Nonfiction for Young Adults: From Delight to Wisdom* (pp. 177–205). Phoenix, AZ: Oryx Press.

Cole, P. (2009). *Young Adult Literature in the 21st Century.* New York, NY: McGraw-Hill.

Coombs, D. (2013). Fiction and nonfiction: A symbiotic relationship. *The ALAN Review, 41*(1), 7–15.

Daniels, H. (2002). Expository text in literature circles. *Voices from the Middle, 9*(4), 7–14.

Fang, Z. (2013). Disciplinary literacy in science: Developing science literacy through trade books. *The Journal of Adolescent and Adult Literacy, 57*(4), 274–78.

Galda, L., and Cullinan, B. E. (1991). Literature for literacy: What research says about the benefits of using trade books in the classroom. In J. Flood, J. M. Jensen,

D. Lapp, and J. R. Squire (Eds.), *Handbook of Research on Teaching the English Language Arts* (pp. 529–35). New York: Macmillan Publishing Company.

Giblin, J. C. (1993). Exciting nonfiction. In S. Sebesta and K. Donelson (Eds.), *Inspiring Literacy: Literature for Children and Young Adults* (pp. 51–58). New Brunswick, NJ: Transaction Publishers.

Harvey, S. (1998). *Nonfiction Matters: Reading, Writing, and Research in Grades 3-8*. York, Maine: Stenhouse Publishers.

Hirth, P. (2002). What's the truth about nonfiction? *The English Journal, 91*(4), 20–22.

Kirby, D. L., and Kirby, D. (2010). Contemporary memoir: A 21st-century genre ideal for teens. *English Journal, 99*(4), 22–29.

Lamb, M. R. (2010). Teaching nonfiction through rhetorical reading. *English Journal, 99*(4), 43–49.

McKeller, Danica (2013). *Girls Get Curves: Geometry Takes Shape*. New York, NY: Plume.

Meltzer, M. (1994). *Nonfiction for the Classroom: On Writing, History, and Social Responsibility*. New York, NY: Teachers College Press.

Moss, B., Leone, S., and Dipillo, M. L. (1997). Exploring the literature of fact: Linking reading and writing through information trade books. *Language Arts, 74*(6), 418–29.

National Governors Association Center for Best Practices (2010). "Common Core State Standards." Council of Chief State School Officers, Washington DC.

National Governors Association Center for Best Practices & Council of Chief State School Officers (2010). *Common Core State Standards for English Language Arts and Literacy in History/social Studies, Science, and Technical Subjects*. Washington, DC: Authors.

Palmer, R. G., and Stewart, R. A. (1997). Nonfiction trade books in content area instruction: Realities and potential. *Journal of Adolescent & Adult Literacy, 40*(8), 630–41.

Shanahan, T., and Shanahan, C. (2008). Teaching disciplinary literacy to adolescents: Rethinking content-area literacy. *Harvard Educational Review, 78*(1), 40–59.

Sullivan, E. (2001). Some teens prefer the real thing: The case for young adult nonfiction. *English Journal, 90*(3), 43–47.

Welsh, K. (2014). Using nonfiction texts to teach resistance in a democratic society. *English Journal, 103*(5), 42–46.

Young, T. A., and Moss, B. (2006). Nonfiction in the classroom library: A literacy necessity. *Childhood Education, 82*(4), 207–12.

Young, T. A., Moss, B., and Cornwell, L. (2007). The classroom library: A place for nonfiction, nonfiction in its place. *The Classroom Library, 48*(1), 1–18.

Chapter 2

An Integrated Curricular Vision

Building Content Knowledge through Textual Connections, Close Reading, and Research Strategies

Rachel Wadham

Inherent in the Common Core Standards (Common Core State Standards Initiative [CCSSI], 2010) is the belief that teaching the skills of reading, writing, speaking, and listening is no longer just the realm of English Language Arts (ELA) classrooms. The Core makes it clear that these skills must extend into all the content areas, including social studies.

While not a wholly new approach, the emphasis on an integrated curricular vision offers challenges for content area teachers. The convergence of communication skills traditionally taught in English and subject-specific content knowledge can be tricky for teachers who have had little training in how to instruct reading and writing. To achieve concinnity, practitioners must learn new skills and pedagogies to successfully address the Core's integrated vision.

Certainly one of the best strategies to start building the necessary skills and pedagogies that will successfully address the Core's integrated vision is to begin with something familiar. For social studies teachers, one of the most familiar strategies is research. Without a doubt, this area is familiar because the quintessential research paper has been a staple in most classrooms for decades.

Since this is a very familiar process, it provides a great foundation to start building a new understanding of the Core's expectations. It is very clear that research is foundational to the Core and the skills associated with research are embedded throughout the Core. "The need to conduct research and to produce and consume media is embedded into every aspect of today's curriculum. In like fashion, research and media skills and understandings are embedded throughout the Standards rather than treated in a separate section" (CCSSI, 2010, p. 4).

Embedding these skills throughout the Core shows teachers just how important these skills are for the type of college and career readiness the

Core hopes to achieve. If this statement does not indicate the importance of research skills in the Core sufficiently, the point is further emphasized in the Anchor Standard for Writing number seven which asks that students be able to "conduct short as well as more sustained research projects based on focused questions, demonstrating understanding of the subject under investigation" (CCSSI, 2010, p. 41).

So with social studies teachers' tacit familiarity with research and the Core's emphasis on it, envisioning how research can be used in social studies curricula provides a strong foundation for integrating reading and writing into a discipline-specific context.

Under the Core's expectations, how we define and present research strategies and projects in the classroom has the potential to look very different than what is currently being done. One need only note the qualifiers that are offered in the standard to see what the Core intends for research. The Core requires that research projects be "based on focused questions" (CCSSI, 2010, p. 41) and the outcome should demonstrate "understanding of the subject under investigation" (CCSSI, 2010, p. 41). These statements show that research under the Core is expected to be much more engaging and in depth than might have been considered before.

First, students will be asked to ask and answer intensive focused questions as they research. This approach seems to preclude the pedantic forms of research that may have been done in the past to produce informational essays on broad topics like "the civil war" or "violence on television."

Secondly, this type of research also requires students to gain understanding. This means that the expectation will be for students to create knowledge of their own instead of just regurgitating what others have said before them. Under these conditions, there is little doubt that the type of research that the Core requires is significantly different than the type of research that goes on in many classrooms today. Understanding this, the fundamental question becomes: What should an integrated vision of research in social studies classrooms look like when based in the reading and writing skills of the Core?

To answer this question and build a vision of what Core-based research will look like, start by breaking down Grade Level Standards for Writing seven and eight required for 11th and 12th graders:

> Conduct short as well as more sustained research projects to answer a question (including a self-generated question) or solve a problem; narrow or broaden the inquiry when appropriate; synthesize multiple sources on the subject, demonstrating understanding of the subject under investigation.

> Gather relevant information from multiple authoritative print and digital sources, using advanced searches effectively; assess the strengths and

limitations of each source in terms of the task, purpose, and audience; integrate information into the text selectively to maintain the flow of ideas, avoiding plagiarism and overreliance on any one source and following a standard format for citation. (CCSSI, 2010, p. 41)

The major verbs from these two standards are: Question; Narrow; Synthesize; Gather; Assess; Integrate. These verbs will be familiar to most as they truly encompass the process of research and represent the major skills required of any student engaged in a process of inquiry. Thus the fundamental process of research required by the Core is an inquiry-based research process. So how can this type of process be implemented into a social studies classroom?

An answer to this question reveals itself by addressing the particulars of each skill in an order that seems to represent a more logical flow than that given in the standards: Question, Narrow, Gather, Synthesize, Assess, Integrate. Since the research process is complex and the steps almost always seem to be recursive it seems unfair to discuss each step in this manner, but this logical arrangement works to conceptualize the process in a more concrete way, thus providing an important mental model that outweighs the risks of oversimplifying the issue.

Additionally, in answering this question, note that the approach offered here is certainly only one possible way that research can be conceptualized under the Core. There will and should be other ways to apply the Core Standards with a wide variety of pedagogies and tools. In fact, one of the most exciting things about the Core is its ability to provide standards while still embracing the complexities of each classroom and allowing teachers to discover and apply the best implementations.

Provided here is only one way, however no matter what form research ultimately takes, this vision should help to expand and enhance the way research is thought about and approached in the classroom. It is also important to mention that the inquiry-based research process has also been very purposefully articulated in the American Association of School Librarians Standards for the Twenty-first Century Learner (http://www.ala.org/aasl/standards-guidelines/learning-standards). This document provides interesting reading for those wishing to explore further.

CONDUCT RESEARCH TO ANSWER A QUESTION

At the most fundamental level, the process of inquiry is centered on the exploration of meaningful questions. Additionally, questions are foundational for building the essential college and workplace readiness skill of critical thinking encompassed in the entire Core, since critical thinking naturally leads students into deeper learning. Lastly, any conception of research is also centered on the asking and answering of questions.

Thus when implementing the Standards through an inquiry-based research process in a social studies classroom, teachers will find that questions become the center of instruction that gives both teachers and learners an authentic context to explore (Langer, 1995; Marzano, Pickering, and Pollock, 2001; Nystrand, 1997; Wilhelm, 2007). However, questions that are focused enough for the Core to achieve the type and level of understanding that it requires, will look very different than many of the questions already in use for classroom research. So what would Core-based research questions look like for a social studies classroom?

The best answer to this is to look toward the characteristics of questions that best engage inquiry learning processes. Grant Wiggins and Jay McTighe (1998) note that to be effective questions that guide inquiry should

- address what really matters in a discipline;
- come up time and time again as part of the discipline's conversations;
- raise other equally important questions;
- be able to be answered in a number of different ways; and
- be connected to individuals' interests and lives.

Questions designed with these characteristics in mind will naturally lead to the type of authentically engaged learning that the Core is looking for. However, an additional benefit comes from the fact that these types of questions are also very suited to the learning needs of adolescents. Young adults are very responsive to the world they inhabit and they desire to engage with issues that are relevant to their own issues, experiences, and concerns (Donelson and Nilsen, 2005).

Since adolescents are facing many important questions as they engage in the developmental tasks that help them form their identities, connecting their learning to these interests and needs makes the process of learning more effective. Additionally, the best type of learning happens when a learner is actively engaged in analyzing and questioning and the best inquiry questions tend to lead to more active engagement naturally because they are timeless and connected to real-world issues and concerns (Applefield, Huber, and Moallem, 2001).

One of the best places to start the generation of questions is through the exploration of nonfiction texts. The great expanse and variety of young adult (YA) nonfiction texts today provides teachers with a treasure trove of interesting questions to explore. For example, books like Cynthia Levinson's *We've Got a Job: The 1963 Birmingham Children's March* raises many questions related to the civil rights movement and brings the past and future of race relations in the United States to the fore.

Wheels of Change: How Women Rode the Bicycle to Freedom (With a Few Flat Tires Along the Way), by Sue Macy, engages with the intriguing questions of how one invention could impact the greater social issue of women's rights. Each of these texts, and many others like them, serve as the best platform for beginning the inquiry process. Thus, the first step for discovering important questions on which to base inquiry-based research projects in a social studies classroom would be to determine a general topic and then locate a nonfiction text that is so engaging that it will draw students in.

Nonfiction book awards such as the National Council of Teachers of English Orbis Pictus Award for Outstanding Nonfiction for Children (http://www.ncte.org/awards/orbispictus) and the Young Adult Library Services Association Award for Excellence in Nonfiction for Young Adults (http://www.ala.org/yalsa/nonfiction) will prove to be great places to start in identifying such texts. A reading of the entire text or excerpts from it by individual students or by the whole class will certainly generate a great variety of rather broad but interesting questions.

Because nonfiction texts represent one author's view, any questions that come from a text will almost always be open to a variety of interpretive avenues for students to explore. Additionally, since any one text can only examine a limited amount of information, questions generated from texts will not be constraining or limited. Also, since authors of great YA nonfiction strive to avoid any biases, these texts will provide questions that will not predispose students to any one type of avenue for inquiry.

For example, a question that directly derives from the reading of *Almost Astronauts: 13 Women Who Dared to Dream* by Tanya Lee Stone, "What does it take to be an astronaut?" can lead to the specific question of: How can cultural norms prevent people from seeing the potential of others around them? These types of questions provide just the right kind of foundation needed for engaging in inquiry-based research.

NARROWING THE INQUIRY

Reading engaging YA nonfiction can generate questions, but for these questions to be suitable for research they need to be narrowed. One important thing to understand is that in order to sufficiently narrow an issue into a manageable research scope, a sufficient amount of background knowledge is needed. This concept of background knowledge and how it impacts the learning process is an important issue in the Core.

Fundamental to the Core is the idea that learners should engage with increasingly complex texts. If it is expected that texts increase in complexity, then there must be a way to judge that complexity and the Core outlines this

method fully in its Appendix A. One of the main criteria, both in the qualitative and reader and task elements of the Core's three-tiered model of text
complexity outlined in Appendix A, is an understanding that texts demand
some knowledge of the reader.

The contention here is that the transaction of reading is as much an inter-
action between what experiences and expertise a reader brings to the text as
what the text has to offer alone. The Core's emphasis on the knowledge a
text demands a reader must have underscores the fact that in order to fully
engage in content area learning a certain amount of background knowledge
is required.

While the Core focuses on the issues of textual background knowledge for
determining text complexity, the same principles hold true for inquiry-based
research. The right amount of background information helps researchers
focus their ideas, pinpoint areas of study, and reduce larger ideas into smaller
ones.

Using YA nonfiction as a base for starting research is twofold, not only
does it help to generate questions but it also provides some of the necessary
background knowledge that students will need to narrow and focus research
topics. For example, the book *At Home in Her Tomb: Lady Dai and the
Ancient Chinese Treasures of Mawangdui* by Christine Liu-Perkins raises
many interesting questions related both to archeological finds and ancient
governments. Narrowing a focus to research further about the Han dynasty in
China would be difficult without the necessary background information. This
text, however, offers that information in a concise way that prepares students
to engage in further inquiry about the topic.

GATHERING RELEVANT INFORMATION

One foundational belief of the Core is that a single text cannot be fully understood in isolation and that it takes numerous texts working together to build
understanding. This idea is clearly conveyed in Anchor Standard for Reading
number nine which states, "Analyze how two or more texts address similar
themes or topics in order to build knowledge or compare the approaches that
authors take" (CCSSI, 2010, p. 35). This purpose is also conveyed in the
Anchor Standard for Writing number nine which asks students to "draw evidence from literary or informational texts to support analysis, reflection, and
research" (CCSSI, 2010, p. 41).

Additionally, the Core does not limit the types or formats of texts. In fact,
the Core expands the concept of texts stating that students should "integrate
and evaluate content presented in diverse media and formats, including visually and quantitatively, as well as in words" (CCSSI, 2010, p. 35). All of this

shows that the Core is asking students to be able to analyze, integrate, and evaluate a wide range of texts, including YA fiction, YA nonfiction, primary source material, scholarly articles, newspapers, magazines, videos, websites, and even multimodal multimedia texts.

Inquiry-based research is a great way to engage students with a wide range of text and text types since it requires a range of information sources to answer essential questions in the social sciences. Therefore, a main role that research can play in the Core is to provide a context and structure by which texts can be gathered together.

Gathering and connecting texts together is one of the most central tasks of research. There are many ways texts can be linked during the research process; however, one of the most logical connections to YA nonfiction is primary sources. In fact, the Core Literacy Standards for History/Social Studies number nine for 6th to 8th grade states, "Analyze the relationship between a primary and secondary source on the same topic" (CCSSI, 2010, p. 61).

The 9th and 10th grade Standard states "Compare and contrast treatments of the same topic in several primary and secondary sources" (CCSSI, 2010, p. 61). For 11th and 12th grade, the Standard is as follows: "Integrate information from diverse sources, both primary and secondary, into a coherent understanding of an idea or event, noting discrepancies among sources" (CCSSI, 2010, p. 61).

These content area Standards can be addressed by using a piece of YA nonfiction as the secondary source. This text serves as the basis for gathering associated primary sources. Primary sources come in a wide variety of formats, so accessing a variety of texts is effortlessly done because today's digital library movement has made many of these primary sources easily and freely accessible.

The best authors of YA nonfiction use primary sources in their work, so a quick look at the source citations of any text should produce a wide variety of texts that can be accessed. For example, in *Bomb: the Race To Build—and Steal—The World's Most Dangerous Weapon*, Steve Sheinkin draws extensively from the Oppenheimer Hearings that happened in 1954 and addresses the loyalty of the head of the atomic bomb project J. Robert Oppenheimer.

The Internet Archive (archive.org) provides access to the full text of the transcript of the "United States Atomic Energy Commission in the Matter of J. Robert Oppenheimer." These two texts together provide rich textual connections that can be gathered together to answer research questions. Even if primary sources are not quickly accessible from the text itself, discovering sources that have connections is easily done by accessing a number of digital library websites.

For example, for *How the Beatles Changed the World* by Martin W. Sandler, there are many enlightening primary sources. A quick search in the

Digital Public Library of America (dp.la) on "beatles" retrieves 63 texts, 37 images, 18 moving images (which includes education videos, news reports, and interviews), and 2 sound files (one recording and one oral history interview). The same search in the Federal Registry for Educational Excellence (free.ed.gov) brings up 26 results, which include sound recordings, historical museum collections, and newspapers. These examples clearly show the wide range of texts that are easily accessible for teachers and students to gather so they can engage in inquiry-based research. By starting with a YA nonfiction text, students can easily be led to the wide variety of texts in a wide number of formats that the Core requires them to engage with in order to be ready for their future in college and careers.

Synthesize Multiple Sources

After a wide variety of text types have been gathered, these texts must then be synthesized together in order to produce an answer for the question. To glean meaning from the texts, students can engage in a wide variety of reading strategies; however, among these, the one that has been proven to be most useful for inquiry-based research is the process of close reading. The term close reading can be operationalized as a very nebulous concept that encompasses any number of reading strategies that require guiding readers through a focused reading of a text and its structures.

Additionally, the concept of close reading can be more narrowly operationalized as a very specific method for reading advocated for by literary theorists that calls for the intense scrutiny of a very short portion of a text (Lehman and Roberts, 2014). However, any conception of close reading can be condensed to its most simple aspect, which is that close reading is reading with a purpose. In inquiry-based research, this purpose is to create new understanding and knowledge that can then be communicated to others.

In order for students to achieve this purpose, a closer level of reading is needed than would be necessary if a reader was just reading for basic facts. Close reading allows the reader to uncover the layers of meaning a text conveys, and this type of close analysis then leads the reader to develop a deeper level of comprehension. However, the process of research is not just about discovering what the texts have to say. It is also about bringing something of the researcher themselves to the task in order to combine what many texts say and to integrate all this knowledge with their own ideas.

In order to engage in synthesis, a reader needs to first engage deeply with a text, constantly monitoring for understanding while at the same time processing the text through their own understanding to create new knowledge. Paul and Elder (2008) condense this complex process when they note that "when you read, you are reasoning through a text; you are reading for a purpose, using concepts or ideas and assumptions of your own, making inferences, thinking within a personal point of view" (p. 8).

Louise Rosenblatt, the originator of the reader-response theory of literary criticism, was also very focused on this important transaction between a reader and a text. One of Rosenblatt's (1995) contentions is that readers bring much to a text, and during reading, a reader needs to work at understanding what the author has to say while at the same time bringing some of their own ideas to bear on the text. These summaries of the process of synthesis show that engaging with a text is really just a process of blending the knowledge of both a reader and a text. Therefore, close reading, which is a process through which synthesis happens, becomes a very important part of inquiry-based research connected to the Core.

Additionally, close reading is an essential part of what the Core expects overall, not just when it comes to research. The first Anchor Standard for Reading requires students to "read closely to determine what the text says explicitly and to make logical inferences from it" (CCSSI, 2010, p. 35). With this kind of explicit instruction in the Core directed at reading closely, there is yet another reason to instruct close reading processes as part of learning how to synthesize sources during inquiry-based research. Close reading tends to focus on the discovery of text structure and because of this it also becomes a very powerful tool for implementing the Core's research-based Standards.

As Sinatra (2000) notes, teaching text structure "strengthens content understanding and report writing" (p. 266). The Core also makes clear that students must analyze the purpose, structures, and development of individual texts before they can be added to a larger vision of understanding. This approach clearly applies to the Anchor Standard for Reading number three which states that students should "analyze how and why individuals, events, and ideas, develop and interact over the course of the text" (CCSSI, 2010, p. 35) and Anchor Standard for Reading number five which requires readers to "analyze the structure of texts" (CCSSI, 2010, p. 35).

These standards indicate that a close reading of the structure of individual texts is a necessary skill for college and workplace readiness. This is because close reading allows students to establish the foundation that they need to understand and compare the approaches that texts take and begin the synthesis process by permitting multiple texts to converse with one another.

This combination of the Anchor Standards for Reading three and five, with the practice of close reading in an environment of inquiry-based research, is a dynamic process that can lead learners to build content area knowledge. Through close analysis, students can begin "reading with a writer's eye" (Robb, 2004, p. 8). Then the instructor need only leverage this knowledge by engaging with the Standards and research projects so that students can "discover what they know about a topic" (Robb, 2004, p. 9).

The task of close reading becomes a part of the research process by helping students to read carefully in order to understand the words, ideas, and purpose of a text. If readers can understand these elements of a text, they are then most likely ready to think about what the author said. From there, they can integrate these ideas with other texts and their own ideas to finally construct an answer to the research questions they have been exploring.

ASSESS THE STRENGTHS AND LIMITATIONS OF SOURCES

The outcome of inquiry-based research is not intended to be a product that just parrots back information gathered from textual connections and close reading. At its most fundamental, the process of questioning and inquiry requires a deeper level of critical analysis. These analytic skills require that students critically evaluate and assess the sources they have gathered and synthesized. Assessment skills include determining the authority, quality, currency, applicability, and accuracy of information.

The Core Anchor Standards for Writing address these skills specifically when in Standard eight by asking students to "assess the credibility and accuracy of each source" (CCSSI, 2010, p. 41). Additionally, the Core Literacy Standards for History/Social Studies indicate the need to develop analytic skills in Standard six, which outlines that 11th to 12th graders need to "evaluate authors' differing points of view on the same historical event or issue by assessing the authors' claims, reasoning, and evidence" (CCSSI, 2010, p. 61). For 9th and 10th grade, the Standard reads: "Compare the point of view of two or more authors for how they treat the same or similar topics, including which details they include and emphasize in their respective accounts" (CCSSI, 2010, p. 61). Lastly, for 6th to 8th grade, it says, "Identify aspects of a text that reveal an author's point of view or purpose (e.g., loaded language, inclusion or avoidance of particular facts)" (CCSSI, 2010, p. 61). These standards specifically address the need to build critical assessment into the inquiry-based research process.

The critical analysis of sources is supported by the fact that much of YA nonfiction is of high quality. In fact, as acclaimed author of nonfiction Marc Aronson notes, the best authors of nonfiction for youth show students through their writing just how the process works.

> Thus we, like the academic historian, need to let our readers into the process: Where does our information come from? Are there other perspectives? Are our sources reliable? . . . We need to show kids how our claims, our knowledge, are cooked. (Aronson, 2013, n.p.)

So quality nonfiction for young adults first provides readers with a great model of what quality research looks like. Engaging with these sources then provides an accessible foundation where students can begin to hone their critical skills. With this background, classroom instruction is easily added to transfer this basic knowledge into skills that can be applied to the other sources students gather as part of their research process.

INTEGRATE INFORMATION INTO A PRODUCT

The last skill to address in the inquiry-based research process is the cumulating one where students integrate all they have learned into a final product. Note that here the word "product" is used instead of "paper." For centuries, the traditional written research paper has been the culminating form for communicating research results. However, under the Core, this form need not be the only format by which research can be conveyed. Inquiry-based research projects can engage students in writing geared toward a variety of text types and purposes, including argumentative and informative/explanatory.

The Anchor Standards for Writing ask students to communicate in all these forms from Standard one, which asks for students to write arguments; Standard two, which asks for informative and explanatory texts; and Standard three, which calls for narrative writing (CCSSI, 2010, p. 41). Without a doubt, the communication of research can come in all of these forms, thus connecting the outcomes of any inquiry-based research to the skills that the Core asks students to demonstrate. Additionally, the Core Anchor Standard for Writing number six asks that students "Use technology, including the Internet, to produce and publish writing and to interact and collaborate with others" (CCSSI, 2010, p. 41).

So, while the Core asks students to write in a variety of forms, it also asks them to communicate in a variety of formats and to share these products with others. The outcomes produced in inquiry-based research can meet all these demands so research outcomes can be presented in a variety of formats including written, oral, or even visual forms. The challenge here is to disengage the connection between research projects and research papers to embrace the widest possible range of communication forms that the Core asks for.

The vision of research that has been outlined above, as painted by the Core throughout the Standards, shows a much more complex vision of research than might have been considered before. However, using many of the already familiar tools, such as YA nonfiction, connected text sets, and close reading, the skills of inquiry-based research that are articulated in the Core are more easily implemented into the classroom. While there are any number of ways that the skills and tools that have been discussed can be used in the classroom, it seems that starting with a question, gathering text sets, and then developing assignments and assessments that require close reading and a wide range of outputs center on the necessary research skills students need to achieve solidly in the expectations of the Core. To show how these elements might all work together in a practical application, consider this general outline for an inquiry-based research unit.

WOMEN IN WORLD WAR II: AN INQUIRY RESEARCH UNIT

General Question: What was the role of women in World War II? How did these women contribute to the outcome of the war?

Texts:

Atwood, K. J. (2011). *Women Heroes of World War II: 26 Stories of Espionage, Sabotage, Resistance, and Rescue.* Chicago, IL: Chicago Review Press.
Colman, P. (1995). *Rosie the Riveter: Women Working on the Home Front in World War II.* New York: Crown Publishers.
Colman, P. (2002). *Where the Action Was: Women War Correspondents in World War II.* New York: Crown Publishers.
Farrell, M. C. (2014). *Pure Grit: How WWII Nurses in the Pacific Survived Combat and Prison Camp.* New York: Abrams Books for Young Readers.
Gourley, C. (2007). *War, Women, and the News: How Female Journalists Won the Battle to Cover World War II.* New York: Atheneum Books for Young Readers.
Kramer, A. (2009). *Women and War.* Mankato, MI: Sea-to-Sea Publications.
Langley, W. (2002). *Flying Higher: The Women Airforce Service Pilots of World War II.* North Haven, CT: Linnet Books.
Mullenbach, C. (2012). *Double Victory: How African American Women Broke Race and ender Barriers to Help Win World War II.* Chicago, IL: Chicago Review Press.
Nathan, A. (2001). *Yankee Doodle Gals: Women Pilots of World War II.* Washington, DC: National Geographic.
Payment, S. (2004). *American Women Spies of World War II.* New York: Rosen Publishing Group.
Rubin, S. G. (2011). *Irena Sendler and the Children of the Warsaw Ghetto.* New York: Holiday House.
Williams, B. (2005). *Women at War.* Chicago, IL: Heinemann Library.

Additional Sources:

American women in World War II by the History Channel: http://www.history.com/topics/american-women-in-world-war-ii.
Female WWII Pilots: The Original Fly Girls from NPR: http://www.npr.org/2010/03/09/123773525/female-wwii-pilots-the-original-fly-girls.
National WASP World War II Museum: http://waspmuseum.org/.
National Women's History Museum Partners in Winning the War: American Women in World War II: http://www.nwhm.org/online-exhibits/partners/exhibitentrance.html.

Official archive Women Airforce Service Pilots from Texas Women's University Libraries: http://www.twu.edu/library/wasp.asp.

Rosie the Riveter: Women working during World War II by the National Park Service: http://www.nps.gov/pwro/collection/website/rosie.htm.

Women in the U.S. Army: http://www.army.mil/women/pilots.html.

Women in WWII at a Glance from the National WWII Museum: http://www.nation-alww2museum.org/learn/education/for-students/ww2-history/at-a-glance/women-in-ww2.html.

Assignments, Questions, and Assessments:

In Tables 2.1, 2.2, 2.3, 2.4, and 2.5, the Anchor and Grade Level Core Standards are referred to using the same shorthand abbreviations of the Core documentation.

Table 2.1 Portrayals of Women in the War

Assignment	Questions	Assessment
Identify images of women in the war in both print and digital texts. Through close reading determine the answers to the questions.	How were women portrayed in images during the war? What do these images have to say about the time and place? What information do the images give us? What information do they leave out? How do these visual accounts confirm or change our point of view of the accounts in the nonfiction texts we read? (R.6; RL.11–12.6; R.7; RI.6.7; RI.8.7; RI.9–10.7; SL.2).	Compare and contrast propaganda images from real life images. Have students create their own image that captures a theme or idea they have discovered as part of their reading, publish these images online (W.6).

Table 2.2 Comparing Primary Sources to Nonfiction Texts

Assignment	Questions	Assessment
Find a primary source account of a woman during World War II. With close reading, compare and contrast this account with one of the nonfiction accounts (R.9; RL.6.9; RI.6.9; RL.7.9; RI.7.9; RI.8.9).	How are they the same? How are they different? How did the author use words and language to convey the types of emotions that the primary source conveys? (R.4; RL.6.4; RI.6.4; RL.7.4; RI.7.4; RL.8.4; RI.8.4; RL.9–10.4; RI.9–10.4; RL.11–12.4; RI.11–12.4) How did the author use the structure of their text to convey important themes and ideas? How was this different than the structure used in the primary source? (R.5; RL.6.5; RI.6.5; RL.7.5; RL.8.5; RI.8.5; RL.9–10.5; RI.9–10.5; RL.11–12.5; RI.11–12.5) How was the content different or the same? (R.7; RI.6.7; RI.9–10.7).	Have students write their own account (as a nonfiction author would) of one of the events they have been studying (W.3).

Table 2.3 Comparing News Sources to Nonfiction Texts

Assignment	Questions	Assessment
Find one or more newspaper articles that discuss an event in one of the nonfiction texts (W.7). Discover the answers to the questions through close reading.	What is the point of view of each text? How does the purpose and/or point of view of each text shape the content and style of each text? What are their similarities? How are they different? (R.6; RL.6.6; RI.6.6; RL.7.6; RI.7.6; RL.8.6; RI.8.6; RI.9–10.6; RL.11–12.6; RI.11–12.6).	Have the students conduct more research as necessary (W.7); then have the students write about an event from two points of view or in two forms (i.e., one fictionalized (W.3) and one as a newspaper reporter (W.2)).

Table 2.4 Assessing Source Credibility

Assignment	Questions	Assessment
Gather information from a variety of sources—both print and digital—on one event outlined in one of the nonfiction texts. Have students read the texts closely and as they do, develop criteria for assessing credibility of sources.	What makes a source credible? What criteria do we use to assess credibility? (W.8)	Compare and contrast the credibility of each source using those criteria (W.8). Have the students present their findings (SL.4) using digital media (SL.5) to share with fellow students their criteria and how each of the sources met those standards.

Table 2.5 Researching the Roles of Women during the War

Assignment	Questions	Assessment
Have students select one role that women played during the war. Have them conduct sustained research projects on that role (W.7; W.8; W.9).	What roles did women play in the war? How can I find information on those roles? How did that role contribute to the outcome of the war? (W.7; W.8; W.9).	Formulate a claim about how this role contributed to the outcome of the war. Have students write arguments to support that claim (W.1; W.4) using evidence from their research to back up that claim.

IN CONCLUSION

It is very clear that research is foundational to the Core and the skills associated with research are embedded throughout the Core. Thus with any Core implementation, research and the skills associated with it need to be fully integrated into the curriculum. Under the Core's expectations, how we define and present research strategies and forms in the classroom has the potential to look very different than what is currently being done. Gone are the days when research was covered as its own separate unit cumulating in the traditional research paper. There are now so many wonderful opportunities that teachers and students can embrace to make research an integral part of the integrated curricular vision that the Core outlines.

Understanding how inquiry-based research can be used in the social studies provides a strong foundation for implementing the Core in classrooms in such a way that strong connections will be made to reading and writing within a discipline-specific context. In addition to the Core, YA nonfiction provides an excellent foundation for beginning and sustaining the research process. The Core Standards, YA nonfiction along with other texts, strategies of close reading, and research skills provide a perfect combination for building students' content knowledge in social studies.

REFERENCES

Applefield, J. M., Huber, H., and Moallem, M. (2001). Constructivism in theory and practice: Toward a better understanding. *The High School Journal, 84*(2), 35–53.

Aronson, M. (2013). Consider the source: Getting history right. *School Library Journal.* Retrieved from http://www.slj.com/2013/01/opinion/consider-the-source/consider-the-source-getting-history-right/.

Atwood, K. J. (2011). *Women Heroes of World War II: 26 Stories of Espionage, Sabotage, Resistance, and Rescue.* Chicago, IL: Chicago Review Press.

Colman, P. (1995). *Rosie the Riveter: Women Working on the Home Front in World War II.* New York: Crown Publishers.

Colman, P. (2002). *Where the Action Was: Women War Correspondents in World War II.* New York: Crown Publishers.

Common Core State Standards Initiative (CCSSI) (2010). Common core state standards for English language arts & literacy in history/social studies, science, & technical subjects. Retrieved from http://www.corestandards.org/.

Donelson, K. L., and Nilsen, A. P. (2005). *Literature for Today's Young Adults* (7th ed.). Boston: Pearson/Allyn and Bacon.

Farrell, M. C. (2014). *Pure Grit: How WWII Nurses in the Pacific Survived Combat and Prison Camp.* New York: Abrams Books for Young Readers.

Gourley, C. (2007). *War, Women, and the News: How Female Journalists Won the Battle to Cover World War II.* New York: Atheneum Books for Young Readers.

Kramer, A. (2009). *Women and War.* Mankato, MI: Sea-to-Sea Publications.

Langer, J. A. (1995). *Envisioning Literature: Literary Understanding and Literature Instruction.* New York, NY: Teachers College Press.

Langley, W. (2002). *Flying Higher: The Women Airforce Service Pilots of World War II.* North Haven, CT: Linnet Books.

Lehman, C., and Roberts, K. (2014). *Falling in Love with Close Reading: Lessons for Analyzing Texts—and Life.* Portsmouth, NH: Heinemann.

Levinson, C. (2011). *We've Got a Job: The 1963 Birmingham Children's March.* Atlanta, Georgia: Peachtree Publishers.

Liu-Perkins, C. (2014). *At Home in Her Tomb: Lady Dai and the Ancient Chinese Treasures of Mawangdui.* Watertown, MA: Charlesbridge.

Macy, S. (2011). *Wheels of Change: How Women Rode the Bicycle to Freedom (With a Few Flat Tires Along the Way).* Washington, DC: National Geographic.

Marzano, R. J., Pickering, D. J., and Pollock, J. E. (2001). *Classroom Instruction that Works: Research-based Strategies for Increasing Student Achievement.* Alexandria, VA: Association for Supervision and Curriculum Development.

Mullenbach, C. (2012). *Double Victory: How African American Women Broke Race and Gender Barriers to Help Win World War II.* Chicago, IL: Chicago Review Press.

Nathan, A. (2001). *Yankee Goodle Gals: Women Pilots of World War II.* Washington, DC: National Geographic.

Nystrand, M. (1997). *Opening Dialogue: Understanding the Dynamics of Language and Learning in the Classroom.* New York: Teachers College Press.

Paul, R., and Elder, L. (2008). *How to Read a Paragraph: The Art of Close Reading.* Dillon Beach, CA: Foundation for Critical Thinking Press.

Payment, S. (2004). *American Women Spies of World War II.* New York: Rosen Publishing Group.

Robb, L. (2004). *Nonfiction Writing: From the Inside Out.* New York: Scholastic.

Rosenblatt, L. (1995). *Literature as Exploration.* New York: Modern Language Association of American.

Rubin, S. G. (2011). *Irena Sendler and the Children of the Warsaw Ghetto.* New York: Holiday House.

Sandler, M. W. (2014). *How the Beatles Changed the World.* New York: Walker Children's.

Sheinkin, S. (2012). *Bomb: The Race to Build—and Steal—The World's Most Dangerous Weapon.* New York: Roaring Brook Press.

Sinatra, R. C. (2000). Teaching learners to think, read, and write more effectively in content subjects. *Clearing House, 73*(5), 266–73.

Stone, T. L. (2009). *Almost Astronauts: 13 Women Who Dared to Dream.* Somerville, MA: Candlewick Press.

Wiggins, G., and McTighe, J. (1998). *Understanding by Design.* Alexandria, VA: Association for Supervision and Curriculum Development.

Wilhelm, J. D. (2007). *Engaging Readers and Writers with Inquiry.* Jefferson City, MO: Scholastic Teaching Resources

Williams, B. (2005). *Women at War.* Chicago, IL: Heinemann Library.

Chapter 3

Range of Reading and Text Complexity

Bringing Young Adult Historical Fiction to Life with Informational Texts

Melanie K. Hundley, Steven T. Bickmore,
Paul E. Binford, and Jacqueline Bach

Historical young adult (YA) fiction provides middle school students with a living past, rendered in narrative and steeped in the people, events, and emotions of a different time period. While reading *The Watsons Go to Birmingham—1963* (Curtis, 1995) (*Watsons*), the reader feels Kenny's fear that he has lost his sister after the Montgomery church bombing in 1963. This pivotal event in American history becomes more significant because of the emotional connection that readers develop with Kenny and his family. This connection often pushes readers to explore the historical events associated with the text; they search for information to support their growing understanding of history.

This developing connection between story and historical events allows readers to situate and develop their understandings of both; the interdisciplinary approach of combining both novels and historical texts provides a richer context for the students to develop critical thinking skills. The study of historical fiction without the understanding of the time period often creates a disconnection for student readers. Part of this disconnection rests in the different expectations of texts within distinct content areas.

As Shanahan (2012) argued, "Disciplines have different ways of writing and speaking about the world. And because of this, discipline experts approach texts with sets of expectations, reading strategies, and understandings that are firmly grounded in disciplinary knowledge" (p. 71). These different expectations of text—whether reading, writing, or talking about them—keep the content areas firmly separate in students' minds so that they don't look for connections between the *Watsons* in their English class with the discussion of Civil Rights Movement in their social studies (SS) class. Making the connection explicit enriches the reading experiences in both content areas.

The Common Core State Standards (CCSS) places emphasis on the development of disciplinary reading, writing, speaking, and thinking practices. English Language Arts (ELA) and SS teachers are aware of the complexities of text and concepts in their content areas; while they often see the connections between the texts they assign and the content they teach, the students may not. Strengthening the visible link between the two disciplines further develops disciplinary content learning and advances reading and thinking skills.

Lee and Spratley (2010) explained that each "academic discipline or content area presupposes specific kinds of background knowledge about how to read texts in that area, and often requires a particular type of reading" (p. 2). The reading skills required to make sense of a novel are distinct from those required to comprehend historical documents, primary sources, or other nonfiction texts. These skills complement each other and using these texts together allows students to develop rich understandings of both texts. While the ideal situation is that an ELA and an SS teacher will be able to plan together to share their deep content understandings, we realize that this is not always the case. In this chapter, we explore the questions teachers might have about text complexity, how an ELA teacher might approach the historical aspects of a novel, and how an SS teacher might approach its literary aspects.

THE CURRENT CONVERSATION ON USING YA HISTORICAL FICTION WITH THE CCSS

Scholars in the field of YA literature have been quick to point out the potential benefits of incorporating the CCSS with YA literature, especially historical fiction. An examination of the conversation promoting the natural fit of using YA historical fiction in the classroom demonstrates how teachers can use this literature to meet new interdisciplinary standards. Moss (2013) points out that not only do the new standards open up possibilities, but they also are "clearly driving the profession toward more cross-disciplinary teaching" (p. 43). In our work, we argue that YA fiction, especially historical fiction, meets the developmental needs of middle school students (Hundley et al., 2014; Bickmore and Binford, 2013); we also believe that historical fiction can enhance the content area knowledge that high school students need.

In *Integrating YA Historical Literature through the Common Core Standards*, one of the first books dedicated to using YA literature to meet the standards, Wadham and Ostenson (2013) devote a chapter on creating a CCSS-aligned unit using *Out of the Dust* (Hesse, 1997) as an anchor text.

Based on Hesse's novel and an essential theme/question, they create a unit of study for 8th graders to explore the Great Depression. Supplementary fictional and nonfictional texts (both print and non-print versions) "provide depth to our study of fiction as well as provide needed support for the knowledge demands of a text" (p. 217).

But, as Talley (2013) notes in her work on the CCSS's focus on developing critical thinking skills, "finding interdisciplinary materials that can help Language Arts and Social Studies students master these skills can be challenging" (p. 26). She provides a close examination of how to select supplementary readings, especially online sources, to support the teaching of a historical event captured in a book. Latrobe and Drury (2009) provide some useful guidelines for selecting quality YA historical fiction:

- A style that hooks the reader into the historical place, time, and plot
- A writing style that avoids long, cumbersome passages
- Characters with whom adolescents can identify
- Settings, time, and places that entice adolescents into the story
- Historically accurate events
- A chain of evidence that the novel is based on research
- A realistic depiction of the period through careful attention to details of dress, family life, and so on
- A powerful, universal theme that spans time and place (p. 75)

The emerging body of work on the role YA literature can play in meeting the standards will not only perpetuate the ELA and SS teachers' need to construct interdisciplinary units but also challenge them to find new ways of integrating a body of texts in ways that students are able to make historical, cultural, and personal connections. In their collaborative study of ELA and SS teachers reading historical fiction paired with nonfiction texts, Hinton et al. (2014) wonder what the new demands on ELA teachers will be as they teach "disciplinary literacy." Will English teachers be required to collaborate more with their content-area counterparts? Furthermore, our role as ELA and SS teachers will be to not only connect these texts but also connect them with our students' experiences and backgrounds. We will need to bring these texts "alive."

WHAT YA HISTORICAL NOVEL AND WHY?

Texts, whether novels, primary sources, or historical documents, do not exist in isolation; readers do not read in isolation. Teachers do not teach content in isolation. Texts and readers are part of multiple cultural moments.

Greene (1993) explained, "Learning to look through multiple perspectives, young people may be helped to build bridges among themselves; attending to a range of human stories, they may be provoked to heal and to transform" (p. 16).

Collier (1987) stated that "there is no better way to teach history than to embrace potential readers and fling them into a living past" (p. 5). This idea of making the past come alive for readers is at the heart of historical fiction. The definition of historical fiction is somewhat challenging; the easy definition is that it is fiction set in the past. How far in the past does a novel have to be set in order for it to be considered historical? Bucher and Hinton (2009) argue that historical fiction is "a novel that was set in the past (at least one generation of approximately 15 to 20 years) when it was originally written" (pp. 213–14). This definition provides a contrast to other scholars (Nesbeitt, 2002) who believe that the novel must be set at least 50 years in the past to be historical.

The shorter time frame takes into consideration the targeted reading audience of YA novels; for many of them, historical is anything that occurred before they were born.

Nilsen, Blasingame, Donelson, and Nilsen (2013) suggest other important qualifications: "They [historical novels] should be historically accurate and steeped in time and place. . . . Historical novels should give a sense of history's continuity, a feeling for the flow of history from one time into another" (p. 258).

TEXT COMPLEXITY AND THE COMMON CORE

We find that too often those connected to educational concerns don't trust the instincts and expertise of teachers. Advisors, educational leaders, and parent groups focus on a Lexile score, a book list, or an award to establish text complexity; this focus emphasizes vocabulary and sentence structure rather than concepts, genre, or themes. There are comprehension factors that are more complicated than a quantitative language measure, a book list, or an award committee's deliberation. The CCSS are much maligned and misinterpreted. In reality, they offer some clear and coherent guidelines about text complexity.

While they offer a suggested reading list in Appendix B, they also clearly state, "[The novels] expressly do not represent a . . . complete reading list" (National Governors Association, 2010, p. 2). Rather than depending on purely quantitative measures or their own book list, the CCSS guidelines suggest three factors, and *only* one is completely quantitative:

1. The quantitative factor includes readability measures that can be counted and predicted—word and sentence length, frequency of a words use, and text cohesion;
2. The qualitative factor includes levels of meaning, structure, language conventions, and knowledge demands;
3. The third factor, matching reader and task, includes reader variables such as motivation, knowledge, and experience as well as task variables such as the purpose of the reading and the nature of the questions that might be posed by the teacher, the reader, or even the context of the reading within a given lesson plan or unit.

The quantitative factors for evaluating complexity in a text are significant; however, they do not outweigh the qualitative measures and should not be the single tool used to determine text complexity.

While most educators can find the Lexile score or some other quantitative measure of a book's text complexity, we are more concerned with uncovering deeper levels of meaning. The structure, language conventions, and knowledge demands that might indicate that a book should be moved up in grade levels might appear too advanced for a book's given Lexile score. For example, *To Kill a Mockingbird* (Lee, 1960) has a Lexile score of 870L, which would place it at the lower end of the 6–8 grade band (see Table 3.1).

In practice, it is most commonly taught in the 9th and 10th grades in the United States. The quantifiable language usage might suggest that it fits in the lower grade band. An experienced teacher understands that the tone at the beginning of the first chapter is not overly inviting with its mundane history of the Finch family and the settling of the community. In addition, the complex issues of race and class, family structures, child abuse, discussions of disability, drug addiction, and courtroom practices make the book difficult for all but the very mature readers in the 6–8 grade band.

We draw your attention to six YA historical novels in this chapter. Specifically, we look at novels representing historical periods found in many school curricula including, *The Watsons Go to Birmingham-1963* (Curtis, 1995)

Table 3.1 Lexile Bands

Grade Band	Current Lexile Band	"Stretch" Lexile Band*	AGE
K–1	N/A	N/A	5–6
2–3	450L–725L	420L–820L	7–8
4–5	645L–845L	740L–1010L	9–10
6–8	860L–1010L	925L–1185L	11–13
9–10	960L–1115L	1050L–1335L	14–16
11–CCR	1070L–1220L	1185L–1385L	16–18

*Common Core State Standards for English, Language Arts, Appendix A (Additional Information), NGA and CCSSO, 2012

(Watsons), The Outsiders (Hinton, 1967), *Death Coming Up the Hill* (Crowe, 2014), *Inside Out & Back Again* (Lai, 2011), *Bat 6* (Wolff, 1998), and *Number the Stars* (Lowry, 1989). Two of these novels, *Watsons* and *Death Coming Up the Hill*, we discuss in more detail later in the chapter.

The six novels can be divided into three possible pairs with each pair focusing on a period within American history. It seems inevitable that students will be introduced to the themes of race and class in the 1960s, the strains and sacrifices of World War II, and the political impact and social engagement of the Vietnam War on music, college campuses, and on refugees through the United States and other countries. See Table 3.2 for the specific settings of each novel.

THE FIRST PAIRING

The first pairing puts together *Watsons* (Curtis, 1995) and *The Outsiders* (Hinton, 1967). Both are examples of novels that are frequently taught, set in 1960, and represent different aspects of social conflict. Both books have sophisticated levels of text complexity that are often ignored. The *Watsons*, for example, is better understood if students appreciate why the father drives from Michigan to Alabama in one stage instead of stopping overnight. Even Kenny, the novel's narrator, does not recognize why it might be problematic for the African American family to stop and find a motel and a restaurant in the segregated south of 1963. This requires an understanding of the racial tension during the pre-civil rights legislation.

In addition, the novel's tone shifts from comic to a more somber tone after the bombing. Kenny is no longer interested in the antics of the "Weird Watsons." His episode with the whirlpool and the near loss of this sister at the

Table 3.2   Lexile Levels and Settings for Discussed Novels

Title	Author	Lexile	Setting	Pub.	Age
The Watsons Go to Birmingham-1963	Curtis	1000L	1963 Flint, Michigan Birmingham, Alabama	1997	11–14
The Outsiders	Hinton	750L	1965 Oklahoma	1967	11–13
Bat 6	Wolff	930L	Late 1940s Rural Oregon	1998	10–14
Number the Stars	Lowry	670L	1943 Nazi Occupation Copenhagen, Denmark	1989	7–9
Inside Out & Back Again	Lai	800L	1975 Vietnam Alabama	2011	9–11
Death Coming Up the Hill	Crowe	NA	1968 Phoenix, AZ Vietnam	2014	

church bombing both are portrayed with elements of narrative that suggest magical realism. As a result, a younger reader would understand the grief, but an older reader, with a greater reading and life experience, would experience a more nuanced reading and see evaluations about race, class, and social activism in the landscape of the novel.

The Outsiders (Hinton, 1967) is also complex. The novel is a frame narration. It begins where it ends and can function as a stylistic introduction to sophisticated novels like *Heart of Darkness* (Conrad, 1901), *Their Eyes Were Watching God* (Hurston, 2000), and *The Catcher in the Rye* (Salinger, 1951). The reference to Paul Newman in the opening paragraph is increasingly more taxing for each generation of readers and requires a different level of knowledge that can be understood by explanation from the knowing other as Dewey (1938) suggests or through the student's exploration of an allusion; a task that demonstrates an individual's preparedness to expand their own understanding.

The final point of the novel's complexity is that a central theme is embodied in the reader's understanding of Frost's poem, "Nothing Gold Can Stay" (1995). Many middle-grade ELA students are reluctant to embrace poetry, nevertheless, to completely understand a dominant reading of the text a reader is asked to connect Johnny's dying request for Ponyboy to "Stay gold" (p. 130) to the characters' discussion of the poem earlier in the novel. Both novels can be easily read if we focus only on the vocabulary challenges. On the other hand, when considering other aspects of text complexity, each novel can be quite challenging even before they are paired with informational texts that would enhance the historical context of the novels.

THE SECOND PAIRING

The second pair includes *Number the Stars* (Lowry, 1989) and *Bat 6* (Wolff, 1998), whose themes and settings are closely associated with World War II. However, neither is closely associated with the battlefield nor the suffering of American citizens during the actual war. *Number the Stars* is a well-known and frequently taught text and the second, *Bat 6*, while it is not as well-known, is an admirable novel with a sophisticated narrative and demands prior knowledge beyond the suggested Lexile score. Part of the complexity of both novels lies in what the reader must know in order to understand the actions of the characters.

Number the Stars (Lowry, 1989) is textually complex due to the content knowledge base required of its readers. While most students in the United States are expected to know about the country's involvement in World War II and the plight of the Jews in various European countries, it is unlikely that they recognize how Danish Jews were helped by the Danish Resistance and people like Georg Ferdinand Duckwitz, Hans Hedtoft, and Marcus Melchior. It remains a perfect example of a book with a Lexile score of (670L) indicating an age range of 7–9 and a grade range of 3–5. The emotional impact of the subject matter indicates thoughtful consideration about the students assigned to study this book.

Wolff's *Bat 6* (1998) also requires a heightened sense of student knowledge about World War II as it played out on American soil during the war and its immediate aftermath. While many US students know a little about the Internment of Japanese-Americans, they are often unfamiliar with the locations, condition of the camps, recruitment of the young men as soldiers, and loss of personal property. These American citizens lost homes and businesses.

Even fewer students would know about the Civil Liberties Act of 1988 (http://en.wikipedia.org/wiki/Civil_Liberties_Act_of_1988) that provided a reparation payment of $20,000 for each surviving Japanese-American who lived in the camps. In addition, the novel's structure is elevated by being told from the point of view and voices of 21 different people. The possibility of supplemental informational texts that would make both texts accessible and expand the knowledge base and instructional tasks could be quite impressive.

THE THIRD PAIRING

For the final pairing, we selected two novels situated during and after the Vietnam War. Both focus on two distinct influences of the Vietnam War on the American Society. The first novel, *Inside Out & Back Again* (Lai, 2011), won the National Book Award for Young Peoples Literature in 2011. The second novel, *Death Coming Up the Hill* (Crowe, 2014) is a recent novel that records the weekly death count of American soldiers in Vietnam during 1968.

Both novels are written in poetic form. This shift alone causes some students to think that the book is automatically more difficult. In reality, the vocabulary of these verse novels is not overly complex. Rather, it is the novels' form that causes students difficulty. The first, *Inside Out & Back Again* (Lai, 2011) is free verse with a variety of stanza lengths. The setting also requires elevated content knowledge. It begins in Saigon at the beginning of Tet in 1975.

Most students know little about the complicated nature of Saigon as the American involvement in the war ended and Saigon fell to North Vietnamese army. The novel's plot then follows ten-year-old Hà and her family as they become refugees and immigrate to the United States, allowing ample opportunities for including discussions of how to read poetry and informational texts that can help explicate the novel's various settings during 1975.

Crowe's *Death Coming Up the Hill* (2014) is a unique novel written entirely in haiku. The narrative is from the point of view of a seventeen-year-old boy in Phoenix, Arizona during 1968. The novel's historical significance is discussed later. One detail, however, is important in explaining the novel's complexity; a feature that is encapsulated in one haiku on the title page.

976
For the 16,592
In 1968

During that turbulent year, 16,592 American soldiers lost their lives. Crowe tells a story in exactly 976 haiku of seventeen syllables. When you do the math, you realize that you have a story that honors their loss by telling a story in precisely in 16,592 syllables, one for each soldier. The structure is written in chapters that represent each week of the year with the weekly death count as part of the heading. As a result, the loss of American service men underscores the important historical moments that are scattered throughout 1968.

EXPLAINING THE CONNECTION BETWEEN CCSS AND THE YA HISTORICAL NOVEL: UNPACKING THE STANDARDS

Standards focusing on Range of Reading and Level of Text complexity provide guiding principles for overarching themes, historical fiction and informational texts, and activities for both the ELA and SS teacher. Instruction that focuses on having students work with and respond to a literary text and complementary informational texts, including digital ones, that underscore and support the literary text's themes, allusions, background materials, and cultural moments helps make the connection among the students' lives, the texts, and the historical events evident.

In order to do this, both teachers and students need to attend to specific categories: key ideas and details, craft and structure, and integration of knowledge and ideas. The disciplinary expectations of these categories are different but complementary and can be used to support and extend student learning.

Key Ideas and Details

Historical fiction demands that students understand key events and the themes that emerge by paying close attention to what those events might mean to society at the time and what the emerging themes could mean as they read the work today.

Craft and Structure

Craft and structure is often a key focus when examining fiction, but it is used less in the study of informational text even though they come in many different textual structures and formats. For example, determining the point of view is crucial when examining various informational texts that might exhibit different ideological stances or that might have been produced for specific purposes. A first person account is different from a newspaper article and those genre differences highlight elements of literary craft that are key in the CCSS for both readers and writers of texts. In addition, technical words and phrases in charts, graphs, and advertisements can be tricky for students whose primary reading might be fiction.

Integration of Knowledge and Ideas

Integration comes into play at every level of the unit. Adding informational texts to the discussion of a historical novel involves constant acts of comparison and contrast. Students will need to merge the information that is presented in different formats in order to evaluate different arguments.

The rest of this chapter explores how to incorporate the CCSS requirement to include more informational texts using YA historical novels as the central focus of an instructional unit. Specifically, we look at the six historical novels previously discussed, representing historical periods found in many school curricula. These novels serve as distinct demonstrations of the ways that a range of informational texts can be used to supplement learning. We advocate for a more thoroughly conceived mingling of the genre categories present in the CCSS documents in an attempt to create instructional units that dynamically meet academic standards and goals while still addressing the interests and developmental needs of middle and high school students.

TEACHER TO TEACHER

The challenge of integrating YA historical fiction, primary sources, and other informational texts into classrooms is multifaceted. How do we as teachers choose appropriate texts to support our students' disciplinary learning? The goal is not to make an ELA teacher teach history or an SS teacher teach reading and writing; rather, the goal is to use a variety of texts in the content areas that support the students' developing understanding of content. The texts, whether fiction or informational, should be intentionally and purposefully chosen for specific instruction.

In this section, we imagine how an ELA teacher might invite an SS teacher into a discussion about teaching the novel staying focused on the text complexity that an ELA teacher finds important. With the second, we situate how an SS teacher might demonstrate to an ELA teacher how to use a variety of informational texts—primary, secondary, and visual—that would enhance a student's understanding of historical contexts.

ENGLISH LANGUAGE ARTS TEACHER TO SOCIAL STUDIES TEACHER

What novels might offer a well-developed, historically accurate version of an historical event or concept?

The Young Adult Library Association (YALSA) and Assembly for Literature for Adolescents of NCTE (ALAN) are two good sources for YA novel recommendations. Each organization focuses on YA literature and creates lists of quality texts in various categories. They also provide lists of award-winning novels. These organizations are a good place to start for a teacher who is unfamiliar with YA literature.

The Watsons Go to Birmingham—1963 (Curtis, 1995) tells the story of Kenny and his family as they take a trip from their home in Flint, Michigan to visit family in Birmingham, Alabama. The novel takes place during a turbulent time period in the Civil Rights Movement.

How do the characters, interactions, and dialogue contribute to a richer understanding of the historical period?

Kenny describes his family as the "weird Watsons" and recounts events in his daily life. This creates a picture of a loving family; interspersed with these images are comments about race relations in America. For Kenny, these comments aren't personal; they seem to be part of his parents' lives but not his. Kenny doesn't understand the racism that his parents discuss or the images of racial violence on television. He says, "We'd seen the pictures of a bunch of really mad white people with twisted-up faces screaming and giving dirty finger signs to some little Negro kids who were trying to go to school. I'd seen the pictures but I didn't really know how these white people could hate some kids so much" (p. 122). The racism and violence does not become real to him until the church bombing; it becomes intensely personal for him when he finds a shoe like the one his sister Joey wears. Because the readers see the family through Kenny's eyes, this is the moment in which racism and violence become real for them as well. Seeing the horror and destruction through Kenny's eyes and feeling his fear for his sister brings the events of 1963 alive.

How does the way in which the story is told enhance your understanding of the historical time period?

The Watsons Go to Birmingham—1963 provides multiple opportunities to focus on the author's craft. The author uses literary elements such as hyperbole, simile, and metaphor; additionally, he uses foreshadowing and humor to develop the plot. ELA and SS teachers are accustomed to the ways in which novels can be used to address the ideas of author's craft; however, there is not as much attention paid to the use of author's craft in the supplemental texts. The 16th Street Baptist Church bombing, foreshadowed in the title of the novel, occurred on September 15, 1963 in Birmingham, Alabama.

This church was an important site in the Civil Rights Movement as it was frequently used as a meeting place for Martin Luther King, Jr. and other key leaders in the movement. The bombing of the church occurred less than a month after King's powerful "I Have a Dream" speech, delivered in Washington, D.C., on August 23, 1963. King's "I Have a Dream" speech, as well as his "Eulogy for Martyred Children," is a powerful supplemental text for the novel. King's craft as an author and speaker is important to the reading and teaching of these texts.

Like Curtis, King used simile and metaphor to create strong images in the mind of the reader/listener. Additionally, King's use of rhythm and repetition help build and reinforce his argument about racial equality. If teachers juxtapose King's thoughtful and well-constructed argument with the sense of fear and loss that Kenny experiences when he can't find his sister, adolescent readers can develop a deeper understanding of the context of the Civil Rights Movement—both what the movement meant for the country as well as what it meant for individual families.

Both Curtis and King create arguments against racism and violence in their texts; Curtis develops his argument through the story of a family that readers come to identify with and love; King develops his argument through the use of rhetorical devices that lead his audience through key ideas and their beliefs. While *The Watsons Go to Birmingham—1963* may not have a high level of text complexity in its vocabulary or sentence structure, its ideas and themes are extremely complex and often challenging for students to understand. King's speeches are syntactically and conceptually complex and provide ways for teachers to increase the textual complexity of the historical fiction while also providing a framework for understanding the context of the time period. The author's craft in both these texts provides tools for helping readers build reading skills as well as conceptual understandings of the contexts.

Part of the challenge of teaching history and historical fiction is the need for an understanding of not just the event's time period but also the culture of the time period. It is not enough to know that there was a church bombing in 1963; the tragic event has a cultural importance that is pivotal in our understanding of the Civil Rights Movement as well as the world in which we live now. The use of informational texts such as Sitton's (2010, reprint) article "Negro Sitdown Stir Fear of Wide Unrest in South" can be used to bring the knowledge of the events and the time period together.

Here are some possible questions to keep in mind when working with a novel in class:

Key Ideas and Details

1. What is the central idea(s) or information conveyed in the novel? How does the central idea(s) or information get represented in the novel?
2. How do the characters view the key historical events, people, and places in the novel? How do their views change over the course of the novel?
3. How does the use of dialogue or character actions in the novel reveal the emotions, motivations, or significance of the historical events? How do these tools personalize the event?

Craft and Structure

4. How does the way in which the characters in the novel talk about key historical events, people, and places differ from the primary and secondary sources? How do their word choices, tone, or use of figurative language or humor provide additional information or other ways of viewing the time period?
5. What is the character's point of view? What textual evidence reveals or suggests the character's point of view?
6. How does the structure of the text reveal information (e.g., causally, chronologically, sequentially)? How does the author reveal information to the reader that the characters do not know?

Integration of Knowledge and Ideas

7. What passages in the source are fact, opinion, or reasoned judgment?
8. Compare and contrast how the historical event, person, or place is represented in the novel and in a secondary source on the same topic.

9. How does reading about a historical event in another genre add to our understanding of the topic?

SOCIAL STUDIES TEACHER TO ENGLISH LANGUAGE ARTS TEACHER

What people, places, events, and terms provide the historical backdrop for the selected historical fiction novel?

History, like literature, has the potential, as Wineburg (2001) observed, "of humanizing us in ways offered by few other areas in the school curriculum" (p. 5). *Death Coming Up the Hill* (Crowe, 2014), set in the tumultuous year of 1968, is just such a novel. This piece of historical fiction provides numerous opportunities for using informational texts as a means of weaving a more complete understanding of the novel and the Vietnam Era. The story, as told by Ashe, a junior in high school, is written exclusively in haiku. The haunting opening verses of the story beckon the reader to fill the empty spaces in our contextual understanding with meaningful detail:

There's something tidy
in seventeen syllables,
a haiku neatness

that leaves craters of
meaning between the lines but
still communicates

what matters most. I
don't have the time or space
to write more, so I'll

write what needs to be
remembered and leave it to
you to fill in the

gaps if you feel like
it. (p. 1)

Ironically, the author's stylistic decision to tell the story in haiku both invites and compels the reader, to seek additional information about the people, places, events, and terms often fleetingly, but explicitly referenced (see Table 3.3).

What informational texts illuminate these people, places, events, and terms?

Primary sources are firsthand, eyewitness accounts (or testimony) about a historical event. As the building blocks of history, they are the informational texts most likely to offer a view of historical developments from multiple perspectives. Often, although not exclusively, they are documents, such as autobiographies, diaries, government documents, interviews, journals, letters, memorandums, official records, speeches, and telegrams. However, they may also include nondocumentary sources or, as Literacy in History/Social Studies (LHSS) 6–8.7 prefers, "visual information," such as charts, graphs, maps, paintings, photographs, sculptures, and videos. Secondary sources, by contrast, are derivatives; they are descriptions of an event based on primary sources.

How can I find relevant primary sources?

In this digital age, several high quality and educationally focused Internet sites offer a plethora of primary sources. George Mason University (http://historymatters.gmu.edu) sponsors a website "History Matters," which provides links and materials for the teaching of American history. The Library of Congress (www.loc.gov) contains an array of primary sources and allows

Table 3.3   References Found in *Death Coming Up the Hill**

People	Places	Events	Terms
Beatles	Vietnam	The Saigon Execution	Activists
Walter Cronkite	Orangeburg, South Carolina	Walter Cronkite's Vietnam Commentary	Hawk
Martin Luther King, Jr.	Paris	Tet Offensive	Dove
LBJ	Prague	President Lyndon Baines Johnson's Speech to the Nation (March 31, 1968)	Communism
Bobby Kennedy	North Vietnam	Washington, D.C. Riots	Napalm
Richard Nixon	Canada	*Guess Who's Coming to Dinner*	Missing in Action
JFK		*Bonnie and Clyde*	Peacenik
Hubert Humphrey		California Primary	Vietcong
Tommie Smith and John Carlos		Democratic Convention in Chicago	Draft Deferment
			Miscegenation

*The items listed in this table are as they appear in the novel from top to bottom.

searches by format including audio recordings, books, films and videos, legislation, manuscripts, maps, notated music, newspapers, periodicals, personal narratives, photos, prints, and drawings.

Finally, the National Endowment of the Humanities (http://edsitement.neh.gov/subject/history-social-studies) offers nearly 400 SS-related lesson plans often incorporating primary sources. In addition, this site allows you to search for lessons by grade level, subtopic (including themes—such as "common core," people, and place), and duration. These are but a few of the many sites offering informational texts and visual information, which might further the understanding of historical fiction.

How should my students analyze these primary sources?

Primary sources require competent and thoughtful handling before they are used in the reconstruction of past events. In the words of Oscar Handlin et al. (1954), "[The historian] is thus committed, above all else, to the rigorous and unrelenting scrutiny of historical evidence" (p. 22). This "rigorous and unrelenting scrutiny" is suggested by the LHSS, which is organized by levels of document analysis: "Key Ideas and Details," "Craft and Structure," and "Integration of Knowledge and Details."[1] The LHSS standards at the middle level (grades 6–8) can serve as the basis for further informational text inquiries. A layered series of informational text analysis questions, as drawn from these standards, might look something like this:

Key Ideas and Details

1. What is the central idea(s) or information conveyed by this primary or secondary source?
2. What specific textual evidence supports the central idea(s) or information presented in this source?
3. How would you summarize the central idea(s) or information in this source?

Craft and Structure

4. Who is the author or speaker in this source?
5. Is this person writing or speaking in an official capacity or privately?
6. What is the author's point of view? What textual evidence reveals or suggests the author's point of view?

---

[1] An excellent source for informational text analysis worksheets (based on document type, but also including visual information) can be found at The National Archives (www.archives.gov/nae/education/lesson-plans.html).

10. Identify and define the important words and phrases in this source.
11. How does the source present information (e.g., causally, chronologically, sequentially)?

Integration of Knowledge and Ideas

12. What passages in the source are fact, opinion, or reasoned judgment?
13. Compare and contrast a primary and secondary source account on the same topic.
14. How does "visual information" add to our understanding of the topic?

IMPLICATIONS AND CONCLUSIONS

The CCSS, with its emphasis on disciplinary literacy practices, multiple texts, and text complexity, provides ELA and SS teachers with an opportunity to enrich their instruction by using cross-curricular materials. YA historical fiction, a genre already an integral part of the ELA and SS curricula, provides students with stories of a living past; a view of events through the eyes of participants. As a result of the CCSS's push for more informational texts, teachers will, no doubt, be scrambling to find examples of charts, graphs, statistics, first-person accounts of events, as well as other primary sources from multiple academic disciplines. Using YA historical fiction and supporting informational texts enhances disciplinary learning in both ELA and SS classrooms.

REFERENCES

Bickmore, S. T., and Binford, P. E. (2013). On a *roll*: Making cross-curricular connections between English and social studies. *Louisiana English Journal*, 15, 13–25.

Bucher, K. T., and Hinton, K. (2009). *Young Adult Literature: Exploration, Evaluation, and Appreciation* (2nd ed.). Upper Saddle River, NJ: Allyn & Bacon.

Collier, C. (1987). Fact, fiction, and history: The role of the historian, writer, teacher, and reader. *The ALAN Review*, 14(2), 5.

Conrad, J. (1901, May 17, 2002). Heart of Darkness. Retrieved October 15, 2003, from http://www.cwrl.utexas.edu/~benjamin/316kfall/316ktexts/heart.html.

Crowe, C. (2014). *Death Coming Up the Hill*. Boston, MA: Houghton Mifflin Harcourt.

Curtis, C. P. (1995). *The Watsons Go to Birmingham—1963*. New York: Delacorte Press.

Dewey, J. (1938). *Experience and Education*. New York: Simon & Schuster.

Frost, R. (1995). *Collected Poems, Prose & Plays*. New York: Library of America.

Greene, M. (1993). The passions of pluralism: Multiculturalism and the expanding community. *Educational Researcher*, 22(1), 13–18.

Handlin, O., Schlesinger, A. M., Morison, S. E., Merk, F., Schlesinger, Jr., A. E., and Buck, P. H. (1954). *Harvard Guide to American History*. Cambridge, MA: Belknap Press.

Hesse, K. (1997). *Out of the Dust*. New York: Scholastic.

Hinton, K., Suh, Y., Colon-Brown, L., and O'Hearn, M. (2014). Historical fiction in English and social studies classrooms: Is it a natural marriage? *English Journal*, 103(3), 22–27.

Hinton, S. E. (1967). *The Outsiders*. New York: Viking Press.

Hundley, M., Bickmore, S. T., Bach, J., and Binford, P. E. (2014). Enhancing the canon with historical fiction and informational texts: The interdisciplinary connection. *The ALAN Review*, 41(2), 95–101.

Hurston, Z. N. (2000). *Their Eyes Were Watching God* (1st HarperCollins hardcover ed.). New York: HarperCollins.

King, M. L. (1963a). Eulogy for the Martyred Children. Retrieved from http://mlk-kpp01.stanford.edu/index.php/kingpapers/article/eulogy_for_the_martyred_children/.

King, M. L. (1963b). "I Have a Dream," Address delivered at the March on Washington for Jobs and Freedom. Retrieved from http://mlk-kpp01.stanford.edu/kingweb/publications/speeches/address_at_march_on_washington.pdf.

Lai, T. (2011). *Inside Out & Back Again* (1st ed.). New York: Harper.

Latrobe, Kathy H., and Drury, Judy (2009). *Critical Approaches to Young Adult Literature*. Chicago, IL: Neal-Schuman Publishers, Inc.

Lee, C. D., and Spratley, A. (2010). *Reading in the Disciplines: The Challenges of Adolescent Literacy*. New York: Carnegie Corporation of New York.

Lee, H. (1960). *To Kill a Mockingbird*. London: Heinemann.

Lowry, L. (1989). *Number the Stars*. Boston: Houghton Mifflin Co.

Moss, B. (2013). Making the common core text exemplars accessible to middle graders. *Voices from the Middle*, 20(4), 43–46.

National Governors Association Center for Best Practices & Council of Chief State School Officers (2010). Appendix B of *Common Core State Standards for English Language Arts and Literacy in History/Social Studies, Science, and Technical Subjects*. Washington, DC: Authors. Retrieved from http://www.corestandards.org/the-standards.

Nesbeitt, S. (2002). *What are the Rules for Historical Fiction?* (Panel Discussion). Paper presented at the annual conference of the Associated Writing Programs. Accessed March 10, 2005, from www.historicalnovelsociety.com/historyic.htm.

Nilsen, A. P., Blasingame, J., Donelson, K. L., and Nilsen, D. L. F. (2013). *Literature for Today's Young Adults* (9th ed.). Boston: Pearson.

Salinger, J. D. (1951). *The Catcher in the Rye* (1st ed.). Boston: Little, Brown.

Shanahan, Cynthia (2012). How Disciplinary Experts Read. In Tamara L. Jetton, and Cynthia Shanahan (Eds.), *Adolescent Literacy in the Academic Disciplines: General Principles and Practical Strategies* (pp. 69–90). New York, NY: Guilford Press.

Sitton, C. (2010). Birmingham bomb kills 4 negro girls in church; riots flare; 2 boys slain. Retrieved from http://www.nytimes.com/learning/general/onthisday/big/0915.html.

Talley, L. A. (2013). Operation Pied Piper: Historical texts and the CCSS. *The ALAN Review*, 41(1), 26–32.

Wadham, R. L., and Ostenson, J. W. (2013). *Integrating Young Adult Literature through the Common Core State Standards*. Santa Barbara, CA: ABC-CLIO.

Wineburg, Sam (2001). *Historical Thinking and Other Unnatural Acts: Charting the Future of Teaching the Past*. Philadelphia, CA: Temple University Press.

Wolff, V. E. (1998). *Bat 6*. New York: Scholastic Press.

Chapter 4

Analyzing and Integrating

Young Adult Science Books that Foster Interdisciplinary Connections

Kelly Byrne Bull

Both analyzing and integrating offer students valuable methods with which to understand texts. Analyzing prompts readers to ask, how do I break this complex text apart so that its pieces make sense? Integrating requires readers to consider, how do I incorporate multiple texts into a whole that shows my new understanding of concepts read? Each skill constitutes a cognitively complex task that students can perform with the guidance of skilled teachers.

Analysis requires that readers break apart text, identify information, categorize into separate elements, and recognize relationships among ideas. In its most basic form, analysis requires readers to examine the parts in relationship to the whole. The fifth Common Core State Standards (CCSS) Anchor Standard for Reading calls for students to "analyze the structure of texts, including how specific sentences, paragraphs, and larger portions of the text (e.g., a section, chapter, scene, or stanza) relate to each other and the whole" (CCSS, 2010, p. 60). Such analysis prompts the kind of close reading and critical thinking called for in the CCSS for English Language Arts (ELA) and Literacy in History/Social Studies (LHSS), Science, and Technical Subjects.

Almost the inverse of analysis, integration depends upon a reader's ability to synthesize ideas and construct a representation of their new knowledge. Integration requires that readers synthesize or put together information in a coherent, logical manner so as to form a whole. A cognitively complex skill, integration prompts readers to comprehend and connect texts in order to construct a new understanding. The seventh CCSS Anchor Standard for Reading calls for students to "integrate and evaluate content presented in diverse formats and media, including visually and quantitatively, as well as in words." Such integration calls for students to comprehend multiple texts, consider how these texts connect, and then construct a visible way in which to show their new understandings.

It is with these skills of analysis and integration in mind that this chapter offers ways in which English and science teachers can forge connections by incorporating young adult (YA) science literature into interdisciplinary units of study.

AN INTERDISCIPLINARY APPROACH

This chapter builds on the concept of interdisciplinary teaming of English and science. As long-time advocates of content-area inquiry and critical thinking, science teachers who collaborate with ELA teachers can promote effective literacy practices across the high school curriculum. Increasingly, high-quality and award-winning science books written for young adults are available to teachers to pique student interest and develop in-depth understanding of science content.

This Science-English interdisciplinary teaming is supported by multiple stakeholders. *Reading Next* (Biancarosa and Snow, 2006), *Adolescent Literacy: A Position Statement* (IRA, 2012), and the CCSS (National Governors Association Center for Best Practices & Council of Chief State School Officers, 2010) support teachers' efforts to involve adolescents with critical thinking and close reading of complex texts.

With the implementation of the CCSS, teachers across disciplines are responsible for teaching core disciplinary ideas and concepts. The integration of these concepts across disciplines such as English and science offers advantages to both students and teachers. Students are "better able to see and make tangible connections across subjects, and teachers are able to build on one another's ideas, making them more focused, engaged, and confident" (Bull and Dupuis, 2013, p. 34). Such integration offers opportunities for curriculum mapping and close collaborations among science and ELA teachers.

Establishing effective interdisciplinary English-science collaboration necessitates that teachers identify common planning time. Teachers can encourage their administrators to incorporate common planning time into the schedule throughout each month or during professional development days. Such collaborative planning will work to enhance the connections that students are able to make between subject areas, fostering the important CCSS skills of analysis and integration.

A MIDDLE SCHOOL INTERDISCIPLINARY UNIT
THE BRAIN & HUMAN COGNITION

This interdisciplinary unit is centered on the theme of the human brain and cognition, and it involves students in analyzing and integrating YA science texts. Through the reading, writing, listening, and speaking opportunities described here, adolescents are able to make meaning from texts and construct in-depth understandings of science content.

Using three YA science books: *Phineas Gage: A Gruesome but True Story About Brain Science, Descartes' Error*, and *The Great Brain Book*, the activities of this unit prompt students to both analyze and integrate texts in order to develop in-depth, meaningful understandings about the human brain. Firmly grounded in the CCSS standards, this English-science interdisciplinary unit incorporates multimodal texts (film, websites, journal articles, historic primary sources) and interactive technology (Prezi, Glogster, Google Docs) to strengthen and deepen students' learning.

To forge interdisciplinary connections, these activities described in this chapter can take place in both the middle school ELA and science classrooms. The CCSS calls for such integration, and the literature supports how such teaming can benefit student learning (Biancarosa and Snow, 2006; Romance and Vitale, 2011; Bull and Dupuis, 2014). In fact, "language arts teachers using content area texts and content area teachers providing instruction and practice in reading and writing skills specific to their subject area" (Biancarosa and Snow, 2006, p. 4) is an ideal way to strengthen students' literacy and disciplinary knowledge.

This middle school interdisciplinary unit provides ample opportunities for students to analyze individual YA science texts and to integrate all three YA science texts in order to create enduring understandings. For each text, there is an annotation, critical review, and guided reading questions. For the central text of the unit, *Phineas Gage: A Gruesome but True Story About Brain Science*, there is a reading guide and learning activities designed for before, during, and after reading. Post-reading activities involve students in connecting the three texts to integrate their knowledge and show their understandings about the human brain and cognition.

The progression of this unit follows five essential steps that center on analyzing and integrating YA science texts to form in-depth understanding. See Figure 4.1.

Step One	Step Two	Step Three	Step Four	Step Five
Read & **Analyze**	Read & **Analyze**	**Integrate**	Read & **Analyze**	**Integrate**
Descartes' Error	*Phineas Gage: A Gruesome but True Story about Brain Science*	*Descartes' Error* and *Phineas Gage: A Gruesome but True Story about Brain Science*	*The Great Brain Book*	*Descartes' Error* + *Phineas Gage: A Gruesome but True Story about Brain Science* + *The Great Brain Book*

Figure 4.1

Step One: Read and Analyze *Descartes' Error* **(See Figure 4.2 for a review of this book).**

Review of *Descartes' Error* **By Antonio Damasio (Penguin Books, 2005)** Highly-regarded professor and brain expert, Antonio Damasio, links the past and present in this book, showing how the human brain controls social and emotional reasoning. Damasio challenges Descartes' "I think, therefore I am" and gives readers insights into the physical attributes and psychological abilities of the brain. In the first four chapters, Damasio connects Phineas Gage's accident to his own patients who have suffered traumatic brain injury, illustrating how the human brain affects emotions and socialization.

Figure 4.2

Guided Reading Questions for Chapters 1–4

Ch. 1: Unpleasantness in Vermont (Phineas Gage)
Explain the physical and mental damage Gage suffered as a result of this accident.
Ch. 2: Gage's Brain Revealed
Over 100 years after Gage's death, how did scientists determine what regions of his brain were affected?
Ch. 3: A Modern Phineas Gage
Compare/contrast Phineas Gage's decision making in the personal and social domains with Damasio's patient called Elliot.
How does Elliot's performance in lab tests compare with his real-world performance? Why might this be, according to Damasio?
Ch. 4: In Colder Blood
What specific evidence (from patients and animal studies) supports Damasio's conclusions about the brain regions' effects on reasoning and decision making?

Step Two: Read and Analyze *Phineas Gage: A Gruesome but True Story about Brain Science* **(See Figure 4.3 for a review of this book).**

Before Reading:

• View author, John Fleischman discuss this book. http://www.cspanvideo. org/program/171748-1

During Reading:

• Complete the reading guide. See Figure 4.4.
• View the 3-D model of the tamping iron going through Gage's head. http://www.nejm.org/doi/full/10.1056/NEJMicm031024

Review of Phineas Gage: *A Gruesome but True Story about Brain Science*
by John Fleischman (HMH Books for Young Readers, 2004)

Readers learn the story of Phineas Gage, the railroad construction foreman, who in 1848 survived the freak accident of a thirteen-pound metal tamping rod shot through his brain. Fleischman relates this true story in depth and detail, illustrating Gage's accident, physical recovery, and social demise. Comparing the scientific knowledge of the 1800s to contemporary brain research, this book prompts readers to consider how and why Phineas Gage's brain damage affected social and emotional reasoning, but not his intellectual reasoning. Historical photographs, newspaper quotes, and illustrations make this an engaging read for middle school readers.

Figure 4.3

- Learn what projections scientists have made about Phineas Gage's injury based on modern science and technologies (such as the MRIs conducted on right-handed men).

    CNN: The Curious Brain Impalement of Phineas Gage http://thechart. blogs.cnn.com/2012/05/16/reopening-the-case-of-phineas-gage/
- Learn why scientists say that Phineas Gage's case proves how emotion and intellect are linked

    BBC: Phineas Gage: The Man With a Hole in His Head http://www.bbc. co.uk/news/health-12649555

After Reading:

- Read how scientists mapped Gage's brain pathways for the first time.

    http://www.newscientist.com/article/dn21820-phineas-gage-brain-pathways-mapped-for-the-first-time.html
- Just a few years ago, the first photograph of Phineas Gage and his infamous tamping rod was found in Baltimore. Read how ordinary citizens determined this unnamed man to be Gage. Smithsonian's Phineas Gage: Neuroscience's Most Famous Patient

    http://www.smithsonianmag.com/history-archaeology/Phineas-Gage-Neurosciences-Most-Famous-Patient.html
- Collaborate, investigate, utilize technology, compose, and present interdisciplinary understandings.

    With a partner, create a Prezi presentation to share what you have learned about Gage. [*CCSS WRITING STANDARD 6:* Use technology, including the Internet, to produce and publish writing and to interact and collaborate with others. *CCSS SPEAKING AND LISTENING 5:* Make strategic use of digital media and visual displays of data to express information and enhance understanding of presentations. *CCSS READING STANDARD 7:* Integrate and evaluate content presented in diverse formats and media, including visually and quantitatively, as well as in words.]

Reading Guide, *Phineas Gage: A Gruesome but True Story about Brain Science*

Ch: "Horrible Accident" in Vermont
- Describe the context in which this 'horrible accident' took place.
- What do you consider to be surprising about this accident? Why?
- Why is the risk of infection greater for Phineas than it would be today?
- Begin note-taking from the point of view of Dr. Harlow: What does he discover about Phineas Gage?

Ch: What We Thought About How We Thought
- Notice the metaphor that the author uses to describe the brain. How is the brain like a city? Like an address?
- If Phineas Gage's accident had occurred today, what new technologies and discoveries would doctors have to be able to diagnose him? Why are these technologies and discoveries important?
- Continue note-taking from the point of view of Dr. Harlow: What does he discover about Phineas Gage?

Ch: Following Phineas Gage
- What did Phineas Gage do during the last several years of his life?
- How did Gage die?
- What proof do we have of Phineas Gage's accident today? How did we get such proof?
- Continue note-taking from the point of view of Dr. Harlow: What does he discover about Phineas Gage?

Ch: Putting Phineas Together Again
- Explain how physical damage to the brain's frontal cortex affects a person.
- What argument does the author make about what makes people human?
- Finish note-taking from the point of view of Dr. Harlow: What does he discover about Phineas Gage?

Glossary: What words do you think should have been included here that were not?

Resources: Choose one of the resources listed here. Investigate what additional information you can learn about Phineas Gage.

Figure 4.4

Each partner presentation will be critiqued by peer partners [*Anchor Speaking and Listening 3*: Evaluate a speaker's point of view, reasoning, and use of evidence and rhetoric.] Writing Assignment To Show Synthesis: Choice Of Options:

A. Write Gage's story from Dr. Harlow's perspective, using the notes you have taken

[*CCSS WRITING STANDARD 3:* Write narratives to develop real or imagined experiences or events using effective technique, well-chosen details, and well-structured event sequences.

CCSS READING STANDARD 3: Analyze how and why individuals, events, and ideas develop and interact over the course of a text. CCSS Writing 10: Write routinely over extended time frames (time for research, reflection, and revision) and shorter time frames (a single sitting or a day or two) for a range of tasks, purposes, and audiences.]

B. Write a report that details Gage's story. Bring it up to date by proposing what modern science could do for Gage today. [*CCSS WRITING STANDARD 8:* Gather relevant information from multiple print and digital sources, assess the credibility and accuracy of each source, and integrate the information while avoiding plagiarism.]

Extension

Read An *Odd Kind of Fame: Stories of Phineas Gage* by Malcolm Macmillan (2002) to examine the primary source documents from the 1800s.

Step Three: Connecting Texts, *Descartes' Error* and *Phineas Gage*

- What primary sources are included in *Descartes' Error and Phineas Gage?* Explain why primary source material is preferred over secondary sources? Use an Alike but Different Chart to compare and contrast the texts by Fleischman and Damasio. How does audience play a role in the writing of nonfiction. [*CCSS READING STANDARD 9:* Analyze how two or more texts address similar themes or topics in order to build knowledge or to compare the approaches the authors take. *CCSS READING 6:* Assess how point of view or purpose shapes the content and style of a text.]
- If Gage were alive today, what could modern medicine and brain science do for him?

  Refer back to the during-reading and post-reading websites to assist you with this. [*CCSS Writing Standard 9:* Draw evidence from literary or informational texts to support analysis, reflection, and research.]

Step Four: Read three chapters of *The Great Brain Book* (See Figure 4.5 for a review of this book).

Guided Reading for these Chapters

Ch. *A History of That Thing Inside Your Head*
- Identify four historical findings regarding the brain (Egyptians, Greeks, and particular scientists)

Ch. *The Controller and the Connections*
- Explain the cerebrum and its lobes.
- How are emotion and memory stored?

Review of *The Great Brain Book*
by H.P. Newquist & Keith Kasnot (Scholastic, 2005)

Beautiful pictures and illustrations that complement the highly readable text make *The Great Brain Book* a good choice for middle school readers learning about brain science. Examining what we know about the brain both historically and scientifically, this text offers a concise, clearly-written portrait of the physical, social, emotional and intellectual capacities of the human brain.

Figure 4.5

Ch. *Neurons: One Hundred Trillion Connections*
• Why does the author use the metaphor of an electrical storm?
• Explain how neurons, nerves, and sensory and motor functions work together.

Step Five: Integrate Understandings from All Three Texts

• Imagine that you can travel back in time to 1848 when Phineas Gage's accident happened. Who and what would you bring with you to help Gage? Write a two-page proposal explaining what you now know about brain science and how you would use this knowledge to help Gage.

  [*CCSS Writing 4:* Produce clear and coherent writing in which the development, organization, and style are appropriate to task, purpose, and audience.]

  [*CCSS Writing 1*: Write arguments to support claims in an analysis of substantive topics or texts, using valid reasoning and relevant and sufficient evidence.]

• Prepare for a debate on the topic: Changing Phineas Gage's fate. Be prepared to argue both sides of this topic. Dr. Harlow cannot change Gage's fate versus Dr. Harlow can help Gage.

  [*CCSS Speaking and Listening 1:* Prepare for and participate effectively in a range of conversations and collaborations with diverse partners, building on others' ideas and expressing their own clearly and persuasively. Audience members rate the debate's logic.

  CCSS Speaking and Listening 3: Evaluate a speaker's point of view, reasoning, and use of evidence and rhetoric.]

• Create a Glogster that illustrates what you have learned from these three texts about brain science. This should show synthesis: how the ideas fit together to form a whole.

  [*CSS Speaking and Listening 5:* Make strategic use of digital media and visual displays of data to express information and enhance understanding of presentations.

CCSS Writing 6: Use technology, including the Internet, to produce and publish writing and to interact and collaborate with others.]
Websites for Students who Want to Learn More

- *Five Paths to Understanding the Brain*
  http://www.time.com/time/interactive/0,31813,1587830,00.html
- *The secret life of the brain on PBS*
  http://www.pbs.org/wnet/brain/history/
- *The Brain: Our Sense of Self (NIH)*
  http://science.education.nih.gov/supplements/nih4/self/guide/info-brain.htm
- *Inside the Teenage Brain*
  http://www.pbs.org/wgbh/pages/frontline/shows/teenbrain/

In summary, these activities are centered on middle school students analyzing and integrating three YA science texts in order to construct enduring understandings of the human brain and cognition. By investigating these texts in an interdisciplinary way, students are able to construct their disciplinary knowledge and further strengthen their literacy skills. Reading, writing, listening, and speaking activities across both the science and ELA classrooms engage students with multiple ways of knowing and learning.

RESOURCES FOR ADDITIONAL ENGLISH-SCIENCE COLLABORATIONS

In professional development workshops for inservice teachers who are interested in considering how to implement English-science collaborations, the author employs the same important skills of analysis and integration. First, teachers are divided by discipline, placing all of the English teachers in one group and all of the science teachers in another group. In these discipline-specific groups, teachers are asked to *analyze* their curricula: what topics do you cover, and what skills do you teach? On chart paper, each group comes up with an incredibly detailed list, noting specific units of study and the corresponding skills that accompany each unit. The more time teachers are given, the more likely each group is to notice how skills are repeated or sharpened during subsequent units.

Then, the author asks each of the science teachers to share their chart of topics and skills while the English teachers consider possible instances on which they could collaborate. Initially, the titles of science units don't grab their attention, but when the science teachers itemize the skills they teach, the English teachers begin to call out or raise their hands. Here is where the teachers begin to consider how to *integrate* disciplines: a few are always surprised that skills of analysis, deductive reasoning, and even persuasive writing are shared across disciplines.

This discussion offers rich opportunities for both groups to consider specific "spots" in their curriculum where such integration or interdisciplinary teaching would benefit students. Of course, the English teachers have their chance to share their units and skills, too. By then, the room is a little loud because more connections are being made across these two seemingly different disciplines. In the end, teachers are encouraged to continue to analyze additional disciplines to seek out opportunities to integrate curricula and skills. Often, it seems that each teacher has simply been too busy, operating as one teacher said "with blinders on" to what colleagues in various disciplines are teaching. Once teachers identify potential spots for interdisciplinary collaboration, many are eager to pursue them.

For these reasons, the author offers specific topics that lend themselves well to these English-science interdisciplinary units, listing specific YA science texts and accompanying websites that can extend and enrich the curricula. Increasingly, young adult literature (YAL) has grown and expanded to include such a wealth of genres and content, offering incredible interdisciplinary potential. The author's particular interest is in YAL that can be incorporated into various science and ELA classrooms. Although this chapter's sample unit on the human brain and cognition was geared toward middle school students, the following units offer potential for either high school or middle school classrooms.

Evolution

Studying biology seems incomplete without an analysis of common ancestry and the growth, adaptation, and development of organisms. Learning how life on earth began, grew, adapted, differentiated, and evolved into the species that are known today is analyzed through this important unit of study.

YA Graphic Novels

- *Stuff of Life: A Graphic Guide to Genetics and DNA*, Schultz, Cannon and Cannon (Hill and Wang, 2009)
- *Evolution: The Story of Life on Earth*, Jay Hosler (Hill and Wang, 2011)
- *Darwin: A Graphic Biography*, Eugene Byrne and Simon Gurr (Smithsonian Books, 2013)

Websites

- *About Darwin*: http://www.pbs.org/wgbh/evolution/index.html

- Evolution Lessons: http://www.pbs.org/wgbh/evolution/educators/lessons/index.html
- Resources from the National Academies: http://www.nas.edu/evolution/
- Evolution on the Front Line: http://www.aaas.org/news/press_room/evolution/
- PBS Video Series: Evolution—A Journey into Where We're from and Where We're Going: http://www.pbs.org/wgbh/evolution/

Interdisciplinary Teaching Article

- Bull, K. and J. Dupuis. (2013). The role of young adult nonfiction in English and biology classrooms: An interdisciplinary approach to teaching genetics. *The ALAN Review, 41*(1), 33–45.

Genetics

A curricular cousin to evolution, genetics involves the study of genes, heredity, and variation of living organisms. Examining DNA, genes, chromosomes, heredity, and traits, the study of genetics is an intriguing unit for adolescents studying science.

Young Adult Texts

- *Moonbird: A Year on the Wind with the Great Survivor B95*, Phillip Hoose (Farrar, Straus and Giroux, 2012)
- *The Race to Save the Lord God Bird*, Phillip Hoose (Farrar, Straus and Giroux, 2010)
- *The Beak of the Finch: A Story of Evolution in Our Time*, Jonathan Weiner (Vintage, 1995)

Websites

- PBS Nature documentary, *Crash: A Tale of Two Species*
- PBS Evolution: *Finch Beak Data* http://www.pbs.org/wgbh/evolution/library/01/6/l_016_01.html
- *Darwin Adventure: Galapagos Islands land birds* http://www.darwinadventure.com/galapagos-darwin-finches.htm
- *Scientific American Frontiers, Evolving Beaks* PBS: Scientific American Frontiers, Video Archive

Interdisciplinary Teaching Article

- Bull, K. and J. Dupuis. (2014). Nonfiction and interdisciplinary inquiry: Multimodal learning in English and biology. *English Journal, 103*(3), 73–79.

Ecology/Environmentalism

Timely and relevant, the study of ecology and environmentalism prompts students to examine cause and effect, noticing how humans impact the environment and the resulting implications. This discipline examines natural resource use and decision making in order to offer solutions regarding how humans can work toward sustainable management of natural resources.

Young Adult Texts

- *Shipbreaker*, Paolo. Bacigalupi (Little Brown Books for Young Readers, 2011)
- *Going Blue: A Teen Guide to Saving Our Oceans, Lakes, Rivers, & Wetlands*, Cathryn Berger Kaye and Philippe Costeau (Free Spirit, 2011)
- *Heroes of the Environment: True Stories of People Who Are Helping to Protect Our Planet*, Harriet Rohmer (Chronicle Books, 2009)
- *Endangered*, Eliot Schrefer (Scholastic, 2014)

Websites

- *Shipbreaker's* Teacher's Guide: https://www.hachettebookgroup.com/_assets/guides/EG_9780316056212.pdf
- Environmentalism for Teens: http://kids.usa.gov/teens/science/environment/
- The Ocean Project: http://theoceanproject.org/2013/10/one-with-nature-empowering-teens-through-environmentalism/

Epidemiology/Public Health

Uncovering the mystery behind the spread of infectious diseases is an essential component of epidemiology and public health. These particular disciplines examine past and present outbreaks of disease in attempt to prevent future contagions.

Young Adult Texts

- *An American Plague: The Strange and Terrifying Story of the Yellow Fever Epidemic of 1793*, Jim Murphy (Clarion Books, 2003)
- *Deadly*, Julie Chibbaro (Atheneum Books for Young Readers, 2011)
- *Outbreak: Science Seeks Safeguards for Global Health*, Charles Piddock (National Geographic, 2008)
- *Invincible Microbe: Tuberculosis and the Never-Ending Search for a Cure*, Jim Murphy and Allison Blank (Clarion, 2012)

Websites

- *PBS, The Great Fever* http://www.pbs.org/wgbh/amex/fever/peopleevents/e_philadelphia.html
- *Eyewitness to History: Yellow Fever Epidemic* http://www.eyewitnesstohistory.com/yellowfever.htm

Forensics

Paleo-anthropology discoveries intrigue fans of science, history, and mystery. Fossils that document human evolution and artifacts left behind by earlier civilizations offer readers compelling evidence of human history. Examining historic sites, fossils, and artifacts, these texts engage readers and scientists alike.

Young Adult Texts

- *The Skull in the Rock: How A Scientist, A Boy, and Google Earth Opened A New Window on Human Origin*, Marc Aronson and Lee Berger (National Geographic, 2013)
- *Written in Bone*, Sally Walker (Carolrhoda Books, 2009)
- *Their Skeletons Speak: Kennewick Man and the Paleoamerican World*, Sally M. Walker and *Douglas Owsley* (Carolrhoda Books, 2012)
- *Every Bone Tells A Story*, Jill Rubalcaba (Charlesbridge, 2010)
- *Lucy Long Ago*, Catherine Thimmesh (HMH Books for Young Readers, 2009)

Websites

- Smithsonian's National Museum of Natural History http://anthropology.si.edu/writteninbone/
- Jamestowne Society http://www.jamestowne.org/Written_In_Bone.htm
- National Geographic Presents The Skull in the Rock: http://education.nationalgeographic.com/education/media/skull-rock/?ar_a=1

CONCLUSION

The YA science texts presented in this chapter foster interdisciplinary connections between science and ELA classes. Because the sciences and language arts promote critical thinking and disciplinary inquiry, the pairing of these two disciplines can lead to productive learning experiences for students. High-quality and award-winning science books written for young adults can pique student interest and foster in-depth understanding of science content. Pairing such texts with engaging instruction that is standards based develops adolescents' skills in reading, writing, listening, and speaking.

In particular, the CCSS-based reading standards of analyzing and integrating are developed through the sample middle school interdisciplinary unit on the brain and human cognition. To read closely, students must *analyze* or break apart text to determine how pieces make sense. To demonstrate new understandings, students must *integrate* ideas from multiple texts to show how they connect, and then construct a visible way in which to show their new understandings. The interdisciplinary unit on the brain and human cognition offers step-by-step methods to use with three specific YA science texts, guiding students through the process of analyzing and integrating across the disciplines of English and science.

In addition, this chapter offered several topics on which teachers of English and science can collaborate to create interdisciplinary learning for adolescents. Topics such as evolution, genetics, ecology, epidemiology, and forensics can be explored through the YA science texts and accompanying websites listed at the end of this chapter. Such interdisciplinary teaming can initiate rich discussions about the role that YAL can play in fostering adolescents' literacy and content knowledge. Encouraging adolescents to forge connections across disciplines can lead to the kinds of in-depth, meaningful learning experiences that teachers strive to provide for their students.

REFERENCES

Biancarosa, C., and Snow, C. E. (2006). *Reading Next—A Vision for Action and Research in Middle and High School Literacy: A Report to Carnegie Corporation of New York* (2nd ed.). Washington, DC: Alliance for Excellent Education.

Bull, K., and Dupuis, J. (2013). The role of YA nonfiction in English and Biology classrooms: An interdisciplinary approach to teaching genetics. *The ALAN Review, 41*(1), 33–45.

Bull, K., and Dupuis, J. (2014). Nonfiction and interdisciplinary inquiry: Multimodal learning in English and biology. *English Journal, 103*(3), 73–79.

Gibbons, L., Dail, J., and Stallworth, B. (2006). Young adult literature in the English curriculum today: Classroom teachers speak out. *ALAN Review, 33*, 53–61.

International Reading Association (2012). *Adolescent Literacy (Position Statement,* Rev. 2012 ed.). Newark, DE: Author.

National Governors Association Center for Best Practices & Council of Chief State School Officers (2010). *Common Core State Standards for English Language Arts and Literacy in History/Social Studies, Science, and Technical*

Subjects. Washington, DC: Authors. Retrieved from http://www.corestandards. org/the-standards.

Romance, N. R., and Vitale, M. R. (March 2011). *An Integrated Interdisciplinary Model for Accelerating Student Achievement in Science and Reading Comprehension across Grades 3-8: Implications for Research and Practice*. Paper presented at The Society for Research on Educational Effectiveness, Washington, DC.

Chapter 5

Problem Posing and Problem Solving

Using Young Adult Literature to Develop Mathematical Understandings

Trena L. Wilkerson, James Fetterly, and Betty Wood

Young adult (YA) literature provides a unique venue through which students can engage in mathematical thinking. This chapter offers mathematics teachers examples of YA nonfiction literature that provide opportunities for students to explore key mathematical concepts in areas such as numeracy, geometry, measurement, algebra, probability, and data analysis. Using YA nonfiction literature as a launching pad for solving mathematical problem situations that arise within the context of a story, and creating or posing problems based on events in the text engages readers and supports students in making powerful mathematical connections as supported through the mathematics and reading *Common Core State Standards* (CCSS) (National Governors Association Center for Best Practices [NGA] and Council of Chief State School Officers [CCSSO] 2010a, b).

Integrating and incorporating reading as part of a mathematics class is not only beneficial, but also critical for deep understanding and support of learning. Research from as early as the 1920s and 1930s and continuing through the years to present day have supported the teaching of reading and vocabulary to facilitate learning in mathematics and in particular problem solving (Earp, 1970, p. 531; Capraro and Capraro, 2006).

Further use of nonfiction can provide opportunities to involve students in mathematical thinking to support communication through speaking, listening, writing, drawing, discussing, analyzing, and comprehending (Ward, 2009; Kleiman, 1991). A teacher can choose to use the entire book, an excerpt, or, as in the case of chapter books, a chapter for a class to set the stage for exploring a mathematical concept. It is the contention of this author that more use of nonfiction coupled with the implementation of effective reading strategies could be beneficial for learning both mathematics and developing literacy skills and processes. Griffiths and Clyne (1994) very aptly stated,

> In linking mathematics and reading, we are seeing a two-way process. Reading contributes to learning mathematics, and mathematics contributes to understanding what we read. Only if we understand the mathematics will we be able to move into making predictions or discussing implications for the future—processes which are utilitarian as well as creative and imaginative. If we integrate mathematics and reading in this way, we will be setting up contexts for problem solving which integrate social, moral, and mathematical thinking. (p. 55)

While this was written over 20 years ago, it is still true today!

Results from the 2013 National Assessment of Educational Progress (National Center for Education Statistics, 2013) indicate increases from previous years in both mathematics and reading at varying levels across states and that there has been some narrowing of gaps in achievement among certain race/ethnic groups. Even with this growth and narrowing, gaps still remain between reading and mathematics achievement of Whites and other groups such as Black, Hispanic, and American Indian.

While progress is being made across 4th and 8th grade results, much more needs to be done, particularly in moving more students beyond proficient levels to the advanced levels. Integrating mathematics and reading can help students make inferences, read graphs, interpret data, understand the wording of mathematics problems, develop vocabulary, and support problem solving and problem posing, as well as further their achievement and understanding.

Often mathematics teachers have not had specialized training in literacy, and literacy teachers have not had specialized training in mathematics. Thus working together is optimal for both in reaching all students. Phillips and colleagues (Phillips et al., 2009, p. 467) encourage middle school mathematics teachers and literacy specialists to work together to assist students in achieving critical understandings for both mathematics and literacy. In their work with middle school teachers, they found that both mathematics and literacy teachers saw more opportunities to make connections between the two areas, and they also saw the need to work together to assist students in making connections between mathematics and literacy. As a result, both teachers and students were more aware of connections and more collaborative in their work (pp. 467–472).

Mathematics is often cited as a foreign or unfamiliar language for many students (Kenney et al., 2005). While mathematical language may be used at times in an informal way at home, it is the formal mathematical language that is a focus of schooling and proves problematic for many. If this is true, then it is further exacerbated for students whose first language is not the one spoken in the classroom.

What follows is a discussion of three major reasons for using nonfiction YA literature in the mathematics classroom: it aids in developing vocabulary, it activates prior knowledge, and it bridges connections. Background and rationale to support these reasons is provided in this chapter along with specific examples for classroom application.

WHY USE NONFICTION IN MATHEMATICS?

Aids in Developing Vocabulary

Learning and using appropriate vocabulary is essential for students to succeed in the mathematics classroom. This is true whether it is trying to read a mathematics textbook, interpret mathematical symbols, solve a contextual problem or develop reading and literacy processes. In particular, the CCSS for English Language Arts (ELA) and literacy in science and technical subjects for grades 6–8 state (NGA and CCSSO, 2010a):

> CCSS.ELA-Literacy.RST.6–8. Determine the meaning of symbols, key terms, and other domain-specific words and phrases as they are used in a specific scientific or technical context relevant to *grades 6–8 texts and topics*.

Using nonfiction literature in the mathematics class can aid students in reading their mathematics textbooks. Often students face challenges when reading a mathematics text (Barton, Heidema, and Jordan, 2002, pp. 24–27; Kenney et al., 2005; Reehm and Long, 1996). The challenges may include reading level, density of the mathematical concepts, use of symbols, unfamiliar syntax and structure, or deciphering mathematical vocabulary.

In particular, deciphering the meaning of mathematical vocabulary is difficult for many students and poses a barrier to understanding. Often words used in the mathematics classroom have dual meanings when considered in the context of a student's daily life. Examples include words such as *mean, product, odd, prime, factor,* and *operation.* Nonfiction can be used to address vocabulary issues and support student learning as it may provide an informal venue in which to encounter the mathematical vocabulary and a means for contextualizing it at the same time. Nonfiction may provide a familiar context while using new or unfamiliar mathematical vocabulary, or even as a means for reinforcing known mathematical vocabulary. The CCSS (NGA and CCSSO, 2010a) for reading indicate that students need to be able to interpret words and phrases used in texts and be able to analyze them based on the context.

It is essential that students develop an appropriate vocabulary that reflects the nuances of words within a given context. The need for interpretation and analysis within a text is articulated in the reading and language arts CCSS

(NGA and CCSSO, 2010a) and supported through the CCSS (NGA and CCSSO, 2010b) for mathematics. Both sets of standards emphasize the critical need for students to understand mathematics, and the need to be able to articulate that understanding through justification.

A useful resource for classroom teachers with a myriad of ideas and examples (i.e., journaling, creating poetry, and developing word walls) for addressing mathematical vocabulary can be found in *Teaching Mathematics Vocabulary in Context: Windows, Doors, and Secret Pathways* by Miki Murray (2004). It includes numerous activities that can be employed in the mathematics classroom to support vocabulary development as they encounter nonfiction literature.

Nonfiction may also provide a bridge connecting literacy areas such as identifying main ideas, understanding writing principles, and making sense of print to mathematics texts. According to Barton and colleagues (Barton, Heidema, and Jordan, 2002, p. 27), text style affects reading comprehension, and often mathematics texts do not follow specific principles of writing, which makes it difficult for students to make sense of the mathematics in the text.

The CCSS (NGA and CCSSO, 2010a) for reading highlight benchmarks related to identifying key ideas and details in text, analyzing structure of text, and reading informational texts (See Figure 5.1). Steve Jenkins' (1999) *The Top of the World: Climbing Mount Everest* and Harold Roth's (1983) *First Class! The Postal System in Action* are two such examples that have students examine text for specific information as well as analyze details to create and/ or solve problems. Perhaps integrating examples of nonfiction, generating problem-solving situations, and then connecting those ideas to their own mathematics text may provide needed support.

Common Core Readings Standard Connections (NGA and CCSSO, 2010a, 10)
Key Ideas and Details • Read closely to determine what the text says explicitly and to make logical inferences from it; cite specific textual evidence when writing or speaking to support conclusions drawn from the text.
Craft and Structure • Interpret words and phrases as they are used in a text, including determining technical, connotative, and figurative meanings, and analyze how specific word choices shape meaning or tone.
Integration of Knowledge and Ideas • Integrate and evaluate content presented in diverse formats and media, including visually and quantitatively, as well as in words.
Range of Reading and Level of Text Complexity • Read and comprehend complex literary and informational texts independently and proficiently.

Figure 5.1

Not only can words have this level of complexity with making sense of text, but it could also extend to use of symbols within text. Use of symbols appears throughout the CCSS (NGA and CCSSO, 2010b) mathematics standards, thus making it an essential part of mathematical understanding for students. There are many symbols that have mathematical significance that also may appear in other situations for students (Kenney et al., 2005, p. 51; Reehm and Long, 1996, p. 36). Use of nonfiction can provide "teachable moments" to explore symbols, such as ∞ or Δ, and their varied meanings and connotations. Rich discussions with teachers, students, and their peers can occur around these to investigate differentiated meanings examining their mathematical and literary significance.

Several of author David Schwartz's books incorporate mathematical vocabulary and a variety of mathematical symbols that connect literary text and mathematical concepts. These include *G is for Googol* (1998), which is an alphabet book of sorts that highlights mathematical concepts, as well as *If You Hopped Like a Frog* (1999), which explores comparisons of real-life situations and their mathematical implications through proportional reasoning and use of measurements.

Activates Prior Knowledge

Students' understanding of a new mathematical idea or concept is often connected to their prior knowledge. Use of nonfiction offers a way for students to either gain needed prior knowledge of a mathematical topic, or a way to support the activation of prior knowledge that deepens understanding of a mathematical idea or concept. Richardson, Morgan, and Fleener (2012) state as one of twelve foundational principles for reading in the content area: "Learning is influenced by the reader's personal store of experience and knowledge" (p. 6) and is therefore an individualized process.

Meaney and Flett (2006, p. 15), when working with Year 10 mathematics students in Australia, found that students need opportunities to connect what they read to their own experiences as well as to the mathematics they have previously learned. Nonfiction can indeed provide students with additional personal experiences and essential information that can support problem solving and concept development in mathematics.

Activities, such as KWLs, advanced organizers, and concept maps like the Frayer Model (See Figure 5.2), can be used with nonfiction literature in conjunction with the mathematical ideas to be explored (Barton, Heidema, and Jordan, 2002, p. 25; Kenney et al., 2005, p. 18; Reehm and Long, 1996, pp. 35–41; Richardson, Morgan, and Fleener, 2012, p. 63; Vacca, Vacca, and Mraz, 2014, pp. 209–15). These types of activities draw on students' prior knowledge and experiences and support students in making powerful connections between the text and the mathematics as suggested by the CCSS (NGA and CCSSO, 2010b) for reading (See Figure 5.1). Further, they can support connections among written, verbal, and visual encounters to deal with misconceptions, vague meanings, and limited understandings (Kenney et al., 2005; Vacca, Vacca, and Mraz, 2014).

Books such as *If the World Were a Village: A Book About the World's People* (2nd Edition) by David Smith (2011) and *101 Questions and Answers About Backyard Wildlife* by Ann O. Squire (1996) invite students to activate their prior knowledge about science and social studies phenomena and employ mathematical analyses to answer or verify predictions, estimates, and applications. Mathematical concepts addressed include number systems, measurement, and statistics.

BRIDGES CONNECTIONS

Integrating YA nonfiction literature into the mathematics classroom and supporting mathematical understanding in literacy classrooms provides dual opportunities for students to make connections to content, their daily lives, social and environmental issues, and applications in real-world situations that may point them to future careers. Professional education organizations, such as the National Council of Teachers of Mathematics (NCTM) (2000 and 2014), National Council of Teachers of English (NCTE), and the

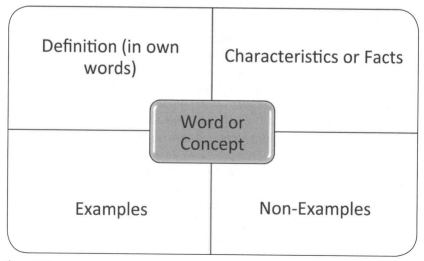

Figure 5.2

International Reading Association (IRA) (1996), support the notion of students making connections, and of teachers being in a position to facilitate the development of those connections.

Further, NCTM points to the connections needed by using multiple representations that include visual, verbal, physical, contextual, and symbolic depictions (NCTM, 2014, pp. 24–25). Nonfiction is a natural way of addressing powerful connections across content and across multiple representations. Specifically, CCSS (NGA and CCSSO, 2010a) for ELA and literacy in science and technical subjects for grades 6–8 supports appropriate connections through text using a variety of visual representations in mathematics.

> CCSS.ELA-Litearcy.RST.6–8. Integrate quantitative or technical information expressed in words in a text with a version of that information expressed visually (e.g., in a flowchart, diagram, model, graph, or table).

Nonfiction provides a context that enriches opportunities for classroom discourse whether it emerges naturally and organically through the use of nonfiction, or if it is well orchestrated by the teacher as described by Smith and Stein (2011) in *5 Practices for Orchestrating Productive Mathematics Discussions*. Smith and Stein identify the practices as *anticipating* student responses, *monitoring* student work, *selecting* specific students to share their work, *sequencing* the selections in a manner to support rich discussions, and *connecting* the responses in relation to the mathematics being developed all with the purpose of organizing rich mathematical discussions in the classroom.

These discussions can help students clarify problems, provide time for sharing their thinking, offer teachers assessment opportunities, and facilitate students' realization that mathematics is a real part of their lives (Kenney et al., 2005; Van de Walle, Karp, and Bay-Williams, 2013). Posamentier and Krulik (2008) advocate problem-solving situations that present authentic experiences going beyond contrived or artificial situations.

Kathryn Lasky's (1994) *The Librarian Who Measured the Earth*, and Kathleen Krull's (1996) *Wilma Unlimited: How Wilma Rudolph Became the World's Fastest Woman*, both provide examples of YA nonfiction that give students literary opportunities in making connections to their own lives, to the world around them, and among mathematical concepts related to geometry and measurement.

Furthermore, and perhaps an even more powerful connection, is that nonfiction has the potential for students to connect their lives to particular social issues and environmental understandings (Griffiths and Clyne, 2004). Griffiths and Clyne (2004) note that nonfiction can afford students new perspectives, give additional information, and provide answers to their questions. Books such as *Fantastic Book of 1,001 Lists* (Ash, 1999), *101 Questions and Answers About Backyard Wildlife* (Squire, 1996), and *Celebrating Women in Mathematics and Science* (Cooney, 1996) are but a few examples of such nonfiction.

SUPPORTING THE COMMON CORE STATE STANDARDS FOR MATHEMATICAL PRACTICE

Nonfiction literature provides a context for creating mathematical problem-solving situations and supports reading comprehension. Approaching mathematics through nonfiction addresses several of the CCSS (NGA and CCSSO 2010b) Mathematical Practices (Figure 5.3), which are essential for students to develop the level of understanding needed in the twenty-first century.

Predicting is a skill and process that is used in both mathematics and in reading literature. Use of nonfiction can support both the predictions involved in the text and in posing mathematical problems that can be used to develop and apply a variety of mathematical concepts (Kenney et al., 2005; Whitin and Whitin, 2004). These can be mathematical problems created by the teachers or posed by the students. Inclusion of nonfiction literature can give students broader exposure to a wide range of contexts from which to analyze mathematical problems in varied formats.

The Reading Standards for Literacy in Science and Technical Subjects 6–8 (NGA and CCSSO, 2010a, p. 62) support students being able to follow multi-step procedures and understand explanations. According to Meaney and Flett (2006), "Mathematics students need to retrieve information from written word, and also from diagrams and graphs to understand mathematical concepts and to apply the information to a range of different problem situations" (p. 10).

In *The Number Devil: A Mathematical Adventure*, Hans Magnus Enzensberger (1997) explores mathematical ideas such as Pascal's Triangle, the Fibonacci Sequence, imaginary numbers, fractions, and Goldbach's

CCSS-Standards for Mathematical Practice (NGA and CCSSO, 2010b, 6–8)	
MP1	Make sense of problems and persevere in solving them
MP2	Reason abstractly and quantitatively
MP4	Model with mathematics
MP5	Use appropriate tools strategically
MP7	Look for and make use of structure
MP8	Look for and express regularity in repeated reasoning

Figure 5.3

Conjecture that invite opportunities for problem posing and problem solving within the context of an engaging story. Utilizing this book, teachers can support students in developing appropriate mathematical practices. Students are called on to read and make sense of a mathematical problem and to develop perseverance in solving problems.

They can use both written and verbal means for sharing their reasoning and justifications, and have potential opportunities for modeling significant mathematical ideas. Furthermore, problems developed by the teacher can be presented that offer students opportunities to select the appropriate tool, such as pencil and paper, ruler, calculator, or spreadsheet, to aid in solving the problem. Teachers can and should involve students in rigorous mathematics to support their reasoning both analytically and quantitatively (Lannin, Ellis, and Elliot, 2011) while also enhancing their reading interests and processes.

PROBLEM POSING QUESTIONS/TASKS
WITH YOUNG ADULT TEXTS

Because making connections is integral for all disciplines, it is especially important in the learning and understanding of mathematical concepts. The use of YA nonfiction literature provides an organic environment, a touch stone for students of all ages to link literature and history to mathematics. Making literary connections to the content of mathematics is exhilarating for students as well as teachers; it also provides a context for meaningful learning. With the literature, an interconnected relationship between problem posing and curiosity seems to exist, as well as providing an avenue for developing vocabulary, activating prior knowledge, and bridging connections.

What follows below are short passages from YA nonfiction literature with possible mathematical questions posed from the given texts. The mathematics in the questions cannot be extracted from the given passages; nevertheless, the content of the mathematics can be injected into the context to develop meaningful learning that advances erudite vocabulary and activates prior knowledge for rich connections.

Problem Posing Questions/Tasks Using *Titanic: Voices of the Disaster*

Hopkinson, D. (2012). *Titanic: Voices of the Disaster*. New York: Scholastic Press.

The Titanic was almost ready—and a good thing too, since there was less than a week to go. The ship reached Southampton a little after midnight on Friday, April 4. Final preparations began early Friday morning. The ship was loaded with 4,427 tons of coal, adding to the 1,880 tons already on board (Hopkinson, 2012, p. 10).

1. The ship was loaded with 4,427 tons of coal. What is the amount in pounds?
2. At Southampton, 1,880 more tons were added onto the ship. Calculate how many tons of coal are now on the Titanic. What is the percent of increase in the amount of coal?
3. Suppose this calculation is 63 percent of its total capacity. How many more tons of coal could the Titanic carry?
4. The Titanic uses 825 tons of coal per day. How many days could the Titanic have sailed before taking on more coal?
5. The Titanic sailed at an average rate of 23 knots per hour. How many miles did it travel before it sunk to the bottom of the ocean? Remember, 825 tons of coal per day were used on the doomed vessel. How many tons of coal were consumed before sinking?

"Although the Boat Deck could accommodate forty-eight to sixty-four life-boats, the Titanic was sailing with twenty, of various sizes, which could hold a total of 1,178 people. On her maiden voyage, the ship was carrying 2,208 people" (Hopkinson, 2012, p. 32).

1. The Titanic's twenty lifeboats could hold a total of 1,178 people. What was the average number of people on the 20 lifeboats?
2. How many more lifeboats would be necessary to sufficiently rescue all the passengers and crew members numbering 2,208 people?
3. Of the 2,208 at sea on the Titanic, 1,523 souls were swallowed into the icy cold waters of the Atlantic Ocean. What percent survived?
4. In 2012, the Costa Concordia ran aground. Thirty-two of those aboard lost their life. However, if the Costa Concordia had lost the same percentage of lives as the Titanic, how many of the 4,200 people aboard would have lost their lives? (Refer to Figure 5.4 for this question).

The first class dining salon could seat more than 550—it was the largest room on board any ship afloat at the time, 113 feet long and reaching across the full width of the Titanic. . . . Chairs at 115 tables were adorned with pale green leather and had special pegs to help keep them steady in high seas (Hopkinson, 2012, p. 56).

1. If the area of the first class dining salon was 10,452.5 square feet, what was the full width of the Titanic?
2. How many chairs might have been at each table on the Titanic?

Figure 5.4   Costa Concordia: This Italian cruise ship ran aground on a reef off the coast of Tuscany, Italy, in January 2012 and toppled onto its side. Of the 4,200 aboard, 32 died and 64 were injured, according to the Associated Press. The half-submerged ship is still being removed. *Source*: http://www.usnews.com/news/articles/2013/02/14/the-eight-worst-cruise-ship-disasters

3. To accommodate all of the students at your middle school, what would the dimensions of your cafeteria need to be if it was proportional to the dining salon?
4. Given your previous answer, how many tables would there be in your school cafeteria?
5. Assume your cafeteria's dimensions are one-third the size of the Titanic's first class dining salon. What would its area be? How many chairs could be arranged around the walls of your new cafeteria?
6. Now, assume the cafeteria will accommodate only two-fifths of your school population. How many students will it hold? How many tables and chairs would be needed? How many lunch periods would then be required?

Problem Posing Questions/Tasks Using *Going Blue*

Kaye, C. B., and Cousteau, P. (2010). *Going Blue: A Teen Guide to Saving Our Oceans, Lakes, Rivers, & Wetlands*. Minneapolis, MN: Free Spirit Publishing.

"If you are a typical person living in the United States, you use an average of 80 to 100 gallons of water every day" (Kaye and Cousteau, 2010, p. 23).

1. According to the chart on page 23, it requires 132 gallons of water to produce a 2-liter bottle of soda. A can of soda is 12 ounces or 355

milliliters. The average person drinks 597 cans of soda in one year. How much water is required to sustain the average person's consumption of soda per year?

2. During your middle school years, how much water is needed to quench your soda quota (assuming you are a typical consumer)?

When you . . .	You use . . .
Flush a toilet	5–7 gallons per flush
Take a shower	7–10 gallons per minute
Fill a bathtub	36–50 gallons
Brush your teeth	10 gallons if the tap is running
Wash your hands	2 gallons if the tap is running

Figure 5.5

1. When you get ready to go to school each morning, assume that you do all or some of the activities listed in Figure 5.5. On an average, how much water do you use each morning?
2. For a given week, how much water would your household use to get ready? Create a table to explain each household member's water usage.

Water is Big Business

Most Americans pay $0.002 per gallon for unfiltered tap water. Filtering tap water with a countertop unit costs $0.025 per gallon and filtering it with a unit under the sink only cost about $0.10 per gallon. Bottled water typically costs about $1 for an 8- to 12-ounce bottle, amounting to more than $10 per gallon (Kaye and Cousteau, 2010, p. 35).

The Mayo Clinic recommends that we consume 64 ounces of water per day.

1. How much would we spend per day on bottled water?
2. How long does it take the typical person to spend $800 on bottled water?
3. Assume that you have a countertop water filter and it costs you $0.025 per gallon to filter the tap water. What is the cost per day for your recommended aquatic libations?
4. How long does it take the typical person to spend $800 with the countertop unit? How long does it take the typical person to spend $800 on unfiltered tap water?
5. If the purchase price of a countertop unit is $100 and it costs $0.025 per gallon to use the filtered water, when is the expense of drinking bottled water the same as drinking the countertop unit?

SUPPORTING MATHEMATICS TEACHERS

The key factor in students being able to understand and achieve in mathematics at the highest levels and to develop the mathematical practices outlined by the CCSS (NGA and CCSSO, 2010b) [Figure 5.3] is effective teaching. The NCTM (2014) purports in *Principles to Action* that "effective teaching is the nonnegotiable core that ensures that all students learn mathematics at high levels and that such teaching requires a range of actions at the state or provincial, district, school, and classroom levels" (p. 4).

Furthermore, teachers should implement tasks and problems that provide students with opportunities to reason and problem solve. One approach is to use nonfiction literature to engage students in problem posing and problem solving. Teachers need access to a wide range of resources to support this approach. While most teacher resources related to ideas for integrating literature (specifically nonfiction) and mathematics are for elementary grades, a growing number are available for teachers of students in the middle grades. These are filled with a variety of nonfiction literature selections with accompanying activities and lesson ideas supporting key concepts in middle grade mathematics and reading CCSS (NGA and CCSSO, 2010a, b). Here are a few titles that are beneficial for teachers to have access either through a school or personal professional library.

- *Math and Nonfiction, Grades 6-8* by Jennifer M. Bay-Williams and Sherri L. Martinie 2009
- *Math and Nonfiction, Grades 3-5* by Stephanie Sheffield and Kathleen Gallagher 2004
- *Exploring Mathematics through Literature: Articles and Lessons for Prekindergarten through Grade 8* edited by Diane Thiessen, 2004
- *Exploring Math with Books Kids Love* by Kathryn Kaczmarski 1998
- *Numeracy and Literacy: Teaching K-8 Mathematics Using Children's Literature* by Robin A. Ward 2007
- *Math and Literature, Grades 6-8* by Jennifer M. Bay-Williams and Sherri L. Martinie 2004
- *Math, Culture, and Popular Media: Activities to Engage Middle School Students Through Film, Literature, and the Internet* by Michaele F. Chappell and Denisse R. Thompson 2009
- *The Magic of a Million: Activity Book* by David M. Schwartz and David J. Whitin 1998

In addition, the NCTM journals *Mathematics Teaching in the Middle School* (MTMS) and *Teaching Children Mathematics* (TCM) have numerous examples of integrating literature and mathematics. They can be accessed through www.nctm.org. A few selections from MTMS are listed below:

- "Locusts for Lunch: Connecting Mathematics, Science, and Literature" by Richard A. Austin, Denise R. Thompson, and Charlene E. Beckmann 2006
- "Making a Million Meaningful" by Kim Ellett 2005
- "John Henry-The Steel Driving Man" by David Murphy and Laura Gulley 2005

Author	Year	Book Title & ISBN	Ratio & Proportional Relationships	The Number System	Operations & Algebraic Thinking	Expressions & Equations	Functions	Measurement & Data	Geometry	Statistics & Probability
Asch, Frank	1976	Popcorn ISBN: 9780819310019	X	X				X		
Ash, Russell	1996	Incredible Comparisons ISBN: 9780789410092	X	X				X	X	
Ash, Russell	1999	Fantastic Book of 1,001 Lists ISBN: 9780789434128			X	X				X
Blatner, David	1997	The Joy of Pi ISBN: 080277562-4	X	X				X	X	
Cooney, Miriam	1996	Celebrating Women in Mathematics and Science ISBN: 9780873534253		X			X		X	X
Enzensberger, Hans Magnus	1997	The Number Devil: A Mathematical Adventure ISBN: 9780805062991	X	X	X	X	X			
Jenkins, Steve	1999	The Top of the World: Climbing Mount Everest ISBN: 978-0618196760						X		X
Krull, Kathleen	1996	Wilma Unlimited: How Wilma Rudolph Became the World's Fastest Woman ISBN: 978-0152012670		X				X		X
Lasky, Kathryn	1994	The Librarian Who Measured the Earth ISBN: 9780316515269						X	X	
Reimer, Luetta & Reimer, Wilbert	1994 1995	Mathematicians are People, Too Vol. 1 & 2 ISBN: 9780866515097 & 0866515097	X	X	X	X	X	X	X	X
Roth, Harold	1983	First Class! The Postal System in Action ISBN: 9780394953847						X	X	

Figure 5.6

Author	Year	Book Title & ISBN	Ratio & Proportional Relationships	The Number System	Operations & Algebraic Thinking	Expressions & Equations	Functions	Measurement & Data	Geometry	Statistics & Probability
Rowland, Morgan	1997	In the Next Three Seconds ISBN: 9780525675515		X				X		X
Schmandt-Besserat, Denise	1999	The History of Counting ISBN: 97806881-41196		X						
Schwartz, David, M.	1985	How Much Is a Million? ISBN: 9780688040497	X	X				X		
Schwartz, David, M.	1989	If You Made A Million ISBN: 9780688070175	X	X						
Schwartz, David, M.	2003	Millions to Measure ISBN: 9780688129161	X					X		
Schwartz, David, M.	1998	G is For Googol ISBN: 9781883672509	X	X	X	X	X	X	X	X
Schwartz, David, M.	1999	On Beyond a Million: An Amazing Math Journey ISBN: 978035322178	X	X				X		
Schwartz, David, M.	1999	If You Hopped Like a Frog ISBN: 9780590098578	X	X				X		
Schwartz, David, M.	2005	If Dogs Were Dinosaurs ISBN: 9780439676126	X	X				X		
Smith, David J.	2011	If the World Were a Village: A Book About the World's People 2nd Edition ISBN: 9781550747797		X						X
Squire, Ann O.	1996	101 Questions and Answers About Backyard Wildlife ISBN: 978082784577						X		X

Figure 5.6 *(Contd)*

CONCLUSION

As a teacher guides and supports students in their journey into mathematics and literacy, it may be that the combination of non-math specific texts (i.e., nonfiction), mathematical applications, and problem solving will facilitate students' development of mathematical concepts, while at the same time extending their literacy skills and processes. More reading and literature experiences in the mathematics classroom can support both mathematical understanding and literacy processes, as well as develop students as mathematical thinkers and analytical readers.

Finally, a sample list of YA nonfiction books addressing mathematical concepts is provided in the Appendix. The listing indicates the major mathematical content areas that might be addressed using the identified book. While these are suggestions, many other nonfiction books exist that address mathematical concepts. Teachers may find that once they begin the instructional practice of using nonfiction in the mathematics classroom and collaborating with their school's reading teachers and librarians or media specialists, many more books will be identified and activities developed!

REFERENCES

Ash, Russell. *Fantastic Book of 1,001 Lists.* New York, NY: DK Publishing, 1999.

Austin, Richard A., Denise R. Thompson, and Charlene E. Beckmann. Locusts for Lunch: Connecting Mathematics, Science, and Literature. *Mathematics Teaching in the Middle School* 12, no. 4 (2006): 182–89.

Barton, Mary Lee, Clare Heidema, and Deborah Jordan. Teaching Reading in Mathematics and Science. *Educational Leadership* 60, no. 3 (November 2002): 24–28.

Bay-Williams, Jennifer M., and Sherri L. Martinie. *Math and Literature, Grades 6-8.* Sausalito, CA: Scholastic, Math Solutions Publications, 2004.

Bay-Williams, Jennifer M., and Sherri L. Martinie. *Math and Nonfiction, Grades 6-8.* Sausalito, CA: Scholastic, Math Solutions Publications, 2009.

Capraro, Robert M., and Mary Margaret Capraro. Are You Really Going to Read Us a Story? Learning Geometry Through Children's Mathematical Literature. *Reading Psychology* 27, no.1 (2006): 21–26.

Chappell, Michaele F., and Denisse R. Thompson. *Math, Culture, and Popular Media: Activities to Engage Middle School Students Through Film, Literature, and the Internet.* Portsmouth, NH: Heinemann, 2009.

Cooney, Miriam (ed.). *Celebrating Women in Mathematics and Science.* Reston, VA: National Council of Teachers of Mathematics, 1996.

Earp, N. Wesley. Observations in Teaching Reading in Mathematics. *Journal of Reading* 13, no. 7 (April 1970): 529–32.

Ellett, Kim. Making a Million Meaningful. *Mathematics Teaching in the Middle School* 10, no. 8 (2005): 416–23.

Enzensberger, Hans Magnus. *The Number Devil: A Mathematical Adventure.* New York: Henry Holt and Company, 1997.

Frayer, Dorothy A., Wayne C. Frederick, and Herbert J. Klausmeier. *A Schema for Testing the Level of Concept Mastery, Technical Report No. 16.* Madison, WI: University of Wisconsin Research and Development Center for Cognitive Learning, 1969.

Griffiths, Rachel, and Margaret Clyne. *Language in the Mathematics Classroom: Talking, Representing, Recording.* Portsmouth, NH: Heinemann, 1994.

Hopkinson, D. *Titanic: Voices of the Disaster.* New York: Scholastic Press, 2012.

Jenkins, Steve. *The Top of the World: Climbing Mount Everest.* New York, NY: Houghton Mifflin Company, 1999.

Kaczmarski, Kathryn. *Exploring Math with Books Kids Love*. Golden, CO: Fulcrum Resources, 1998.

Kaye, C. B., and P. Cousteau. *Going Blue: A Teen Guide to Saving Our Oceans, Lakes, Rivers, & Wetlands*. Minneapolis, MN: Free Spirit Publishing, 2010.

Kenney, Joan M., Euthecia Hancewicz, Loretta Heuer, Diana Metsisto, and Cynthia L. Tuttle. *Literacy Strategies for Improving Mathematics Instruction*. Alexandria, VA: Association for Supervision and Curriculum Development, 2005.

Kleiman, Glenn M. Mathematics across the curriculum. *Educational Leadership* 49, no. 2 (1991): 48–51.

Krull, Kathleen. *Wilma Unlimited: How Wilma Rudolph Became the World's Fastest Woman*. Orlando, FL: Harcourt, Inc., 1996.

Lannin, John, Amy B. Ellis, and Rebekah Elliott. *Developing Essential Understandings of Mathematical Reasoning for Teaching Mathematics in Prekindergarten-Grade 8*. Reston, VA: National Council of Teachers of Mathematics, 2011.

Lasky, Kathryn. *The Librarian Who Measured the Earth*. Hong Kong: South China Printing Company, 1994.

Meaney, Tamsin, and Kirsten Flett. Learning to Read in Mathematics Classrooms. *Australian Mathematics Teacher* 62, no. 2 (2006): 10–16.

Murphy, David, and Laura Gulley. John Henry-The Steel Driving Man. *Mathematics Teaching in the Middle School* 10, no. 8 (2005): 380–85.

Murray, Miki. *Teaching Mathematics Vocabulary in Context: Windows, Doors, and Secret Pathways*. Portsmouth, NH: Heinemann, 2004.

National Center for Education Statistics. *The Nation's Report Card: A First Look: 2013 Mathematics and Reading (NCES 2014-451)*. Washington, DC: Institute of Education Sciences, U.S. Department of Education, 2013.

National Council of Teachers of English (NCTE) and International Reading Association (IRA). *Standards for the English Language Arts*. Urbana, IL: NCTE, 1996.

National Council of Teachers of Mathematics. *Principles and Standards for School Mathematics*. Reston, VA: NCTM, 2000.

National Council of Teachers of Mathematics. *Principles to Action*. Reston, VA: NCTM, 2014.

National Governors Association Center for Best Practices & the Council of Chief State School Officers. *Common Core State Standards for English Language Arts*, 2010a. Retrieved from http://www.corestandards.org/ELA-Literacy/.

National Governors Association Center for Best Practices & the Council of Chief State School Officers. *Common Core State Standards for Mathematics*, 2010b. Retrieved from http://www.corestandards.org/Math/.

Phillips, Donna C. Kester, Mary Ellen Bardsley, Thomas Bach, and Kathleen Gibb-Brown. "But I Teach Math!" The Journey of Middle School Mathematics Teachers and Literacy Coaches Learning to Integrate Strategies into the Math Instruction. *Education* 129 (2009): 467–72.

Posamentier, Alfred S., and Stephen Krulik. *Problem-Solving Strategies for Efficient and Elegant Solutions, Grades 6-12: A Resource for the Mathematics Teacher*. Thousand Oaks, CA: Corwin Press, 2008.

Reehm, Sue P., and Shirley A. Long. Reading in the Mathematics Classroom. *Middle School Journal* 27, no. 5 (May 1996): 35–41.

Richardson, Judy S., Raymond F. Morgan, and Charlene E. Fleener. *Reading to Learn in the Content Areas*, 11th ed. Belmont, CA: Wadsworth Cengage Learning, 2012.

Roth, Harold. *First Class! The Postal System in Action*. New York, NY: Knopf Books for Young Readers, 1983.

Schwartz, David. *G is for Googol*. Berkley: Tricyle Press, 1998.

Schwartz, David. *If You Hopped Like a Frog*. New York: Scholastic, 1999.

Schwartz, David M., and David J. Whitin. *The Magic of a Million: Activity Book*. New York, NY: Scholastic, 1998.

Sheffield, Stephanie, and Kathleen Gallagher. *Math and Nonfiction, Grades 3-5*. Sausalito, CA: Scholastic, Math Solutions Publications, 2004.

Smith, David J. *If the World Were a Village: A Book About the World's People*, 2nd ed. Tonawanda, New York Kids Can Press, Ltd., 2011.

Smith, Margaret S., and Mary Kay Stein. *5 Practices for Orchestrating Productive Mathematics Discussions*. Reston, VA: National Council of Teachers of Mathematics, 2011.

Squire, Ann O. *101 Questions and Answers About Backyard Wildlife*. London: Walker Books Ltd., 1996.

Thiessen, Diane (ed.). *Exploring Mathematics through Literature: Articles and Lessons for Prekindergarten through Grade 8*. Reston, VA: NCTM, 2004.

Vacca, Richard T., Jo Anne Vacca, and Maryann Mraz. *Content Area Reading: Literacy and Learning Across the Curriculum*. Boston: Pearson, 2014.

Van de Walle, John A., Karen S. Karp, and Jennifer M. Bay-Williams. *Elementary and Middle School Mathematics: Teaching Developmentally*, 8th ed. Boston: Pearson, 2013.

Ward, Robin A. *Numeracy and Literacy: Teaching K-8 Mathematics Using Children's Literature*. New York, NY: Guilford Publications, Inc., 2007.

Ward, Robin A. *Literature-based Activities for Integrating Mathematics with Other Content Areas, Grades 3-5*. Boston: Pearson, 2009.

Whitin, David J., and Phyllis Whitin. *New Visions for Linking Literature and Mathematics*. Urbana, IL: National Council of Teachers of English and Reston, VA: National Council of Teachers of Mathematics, 2004.

Chapter 6

Interdisciplinary Opportunities with Young Adult Historical Nonfiction Literature and the Common Core

An Exploration of the Black Freedom Struggle

Susan L. Groenke and Robert Prickett

Harper Lee's classic, Pulitzer Prize-winning, North American novel *To Kill a Mockingbird* (TKAM), published in 1960, sells about a million copies per year, and is consistently ranked in reader surveys as the most influential book in Americans' lives (after, of course, the Bible). Told from the perspective of its female protagonist, eight-year-old Scout Finch, TKAM explores themes of morality, empathy, and coming-of-age against the backdrop of a racial caste system in the Jim Crow South.

The book is consistently taught in North American schools—a tradition we are sure will continue with the Common Core State Standards' adoption of the novel as an "exemplar text." According to the Common Core Standards authors, exemplar texts are those texts that "exemplify the level of complexity and quality that the Standards require all students in a given grade band to engage with," and "should serve as useful guideposts in helping educators select texts of similar complexity, quality, and range for their own classrooms" (CCSS, 2010).

We agree with the assertion that TKAM is a "complex" text, and in this chapter, we offer a strategy—complementary nonfiction literature circles—that secondary English language arts (ELA) teachers can use in their instruction of TKAM. We offer this strategy not only to help teachers meet the Common Core Reading Standards with nonfiction texts, but to also encourage ELA teachers to contextualize TKAM to highlight the black liberation struggle in their instruction.

As Kelley (2010) found in his research on what English teachers say to students about TKAM when they teach the novel: "Teachers are highly attuned to the fictional world created in the novel . . . but few specific references to landmarks in the struggle for African American civil rights (e.g., the Montgomery bus boycott, *Brown v. Board of Education*) [occur]" (p. 11). Race scholar Isaac Saney (2003) explains this as problematic because it "denies the historical agency of Black people":

> The novel and its supporters deny that Black people have been the central actors in their movement for liberation and justice, from widespread African resistance to, and revolts against, slavery and colonialism to the twentieth century's mass movements challenging segregation, discrimination, and imperialism. . . . *To Kill a Mockingbird* gives no inkling of this protest and instead creates the indelible impression that the entire Black community existed in a complete state of paralysis. (p. 103)

We know that African Americans living under Jim Crow in the South did not exist in a "state of paralysis." We have too many witnesses and too much good nonfiction about the black struggle for liberation and civil rights that tells us differently. Though there are increasing examples of TKAM being taught in combination with or focusing on the historical Black Freedom struggle (Hagberg, 2013; Kumler and Palchick, 2008; Maher, 2013; Prince William County Public Schools, 1997; Ricker-Wilson, 1998), we know that traditional instruction of TKAM in high school English classrooms can still be focused predominantly on the sole use of the fictional text and on themes of morality, empathy, and/or coming-of-age (Kelley, 2010). This literary focus on text does not always make room for black voices and perspectives, and thus may not disrupt the idea of African American passivity or paralysis during the Jim Crow era (Saney, 2003).

In addition, traditional instruction of TKAM may not counteract "the powerful negative societal representations of people of color or . . . challenge pervasive and negative dominant-culture depictions about identity," as Carol Ricker-Wilson (1998) found when she taught the novel to a diverse group of Canadian high school students (p. 71). Based on her experiences teaching TKAM, Ricker-Wilson recommends teaching Mildred Taylor's (1972) classic YA novel *Roll of Thunder, Hear My Cry* in conjunction with TKAM because "Taylor focuses on portraying black people as complex beings, subject to weakness, but primarily as emotionally healthy, astute and active resistors and saboteurs of racist actions, individuals and institutions" (p. 72).

In this chapter, we offer the idea of teaching quality nonfiction texts like James Sturm and Rich Tommaso's (2007) graphic biography, *Satchel Paige: Striking Out Jim Crow* (Satchel Paige), and Melba Patillo Beals' (1995) *Warriors Don't Cry: A Searing Memoir of the Battle to Integrate Little Rock's Central High* (Warriors Don't Cry) in conjunction with TKAM for the same reason Ricker-Wilson provides. Unlike the fictional black characters in Taylor's novel, however, the nonfiction we suggest using portrays *real* human beings who actively resisted racist actions and institutions. We think it is important for high school students to know about people like Satchel Paige and Melba Patillo Beals.

In addition, we are feeling the pressure of the Common Core Reading Standards for Informational Texts in our states, with their emphasis on increased reading of nonfiction and informational texts across the school day. While we are aware of the controversy and debates surrounding the standards, best practices in reading instruction, and definitions of "nonfiction," we feel the new standards provide an opportunity for teachers to model how nonfiction can be integrated with fiction in the high school English classroom to meet instructional goals.

For these reasons, in what follows, we describe two works of YA historical nonfiction that we think would make good complementary pairings with TKAM in a small-group nonfiction-literature-circles activity. After we describe these texts, we then explain our use of the texts in a recent summer methods course for beginning high school English teachers. In the course, teachers read TKAM and one of the nonfiction texts of choice, and participated in small-group nonfiction-literature circles. For the purposes of this chapter, we focus on two of the four groups, Group One that read *Striking Out Jim Crow*, and Group Two that read *Warriors Don't Cry*.

DEFINING AND SELECTING GOOD NONFICTION FOR THE SECONDARY ELA CLASSROOM

In his 2002 article "Expository Text in Literature Circles," literature circle guru Harvey Daniels explains that small-group literature circles are a good medium for the reading of nonfiction, but teachers have to be careful about how they both *define* nonfiction and *select* nonfiction to use in small-group literature circle activities. Daniels explains that expository texts can range from "simple, consistent organizational patterns [with] a high proportion of information [e.g., textbooks, manuals, contracts] to those with complex, multiple-organizational patterns and a blend of information and 'story' [e.g., biographies, memoirs, historical novels]" (p. 9).

Daniels suggests that teachers consider more "story-like" expository texts when selecting nonfiction to use in literature circles. He explains:

> We need material that has more than "facts and details." If nonfiction circles are going to be as successful as literature circles, kids need texts that are "discussable," meaning that they have *some* of these ingredients: (1) content that is important or engaging; (2) people we can care about; (3) a narrative structure

or chronological line; (4) places we can visualize; (5) danger, conflicts, risks, or choices; (6) value, moral, ethical, or political dimensions; and (7) some ideas that reasonable people can debate, dispute, or disagree about. (p. 11)

James Sturm and Rich Tommaso's graphic biography, *Satchel Paige: Striking Out Jim Crow*, and Melba Beals Pattillo's *Warriors Don't Cry: A Searing Memoir of the Battle to Integrate Little Rock's Central High* certainly have many of Daniel's ingredients and that's why we chose them. Ultimately, we also chose these nonfiction texts because they provided an accurate, authentic, and engaging black perspective of life under Jim Crow, as well as portrayals of active African American resistance against white supremacy.

HISTORICAL NONFICTION DEPICTING BLACK AGENCY

Satchel Paige: Striking Out Jim Crow

Leroy Robert "Satchel" Paige was an African American pitcher in both the Negro Leagues and the Major Leagues during the Jim Crow era. The graphic novel *Satchel Paige: Striking Out Jim Crow* is, however, less a biography of the famed pitcher and more a story of life as lived by African Americans in the Deep South during Jim Crow. In fact, the well-known historical figure Satchel Paige seems incidental to the story, compared with the fictional protagonist, Emmet, Sr. The graphic novel really tells the story of Emmet, Sr., a fictional sharecropper who leaves his family in 1929 to pursue his dream of playing professional baseball in the Negro Leagues. Blacks were not accepted into the existing white major and minor baseball leagues, so they formed their own teams and baseball leagues—and that was how the Negro Leagues were formed.

When Emmet, Sr.'s dream is literally shattered (through a busted knee injury), he returns to sharecropping on the Jennings' farm (the farm is owned by twin sons, Wallace and William Jennings). Desiring a better life for his son, Emmet, Sr. sends his son, Emmet, Jr., to school. Because he attends school instead of working, Emmet, Jr. is beaten by the Jennings twins. Then one day, advertisements announce that Satchel Paige's team is coming to town to play the local (white) baseball team. The Jennings twins play on the local white team. At first, Paige is a no-show; as the day progresses, however, Paige arrives and is called "a washed-up nigger" by Wallace Jennings when Paige takes his time on the field and jokes around with the players. Paige retaliates by calling in the infield when the Jennings twins are at bat and striking them both out.

The game inspires and empowers Emmet, Sr. and his son, and Emmet, Sr. ultimately tells his son about getting a hit off Satchel Paige when he was a ballplayer. The text ends with Emmet, Sr. thinking: "For the first time since I played ball, since Emmet, Jr. was a baby, I felt somethin' on the inside. I remembered the type of man I am. I gave Emmet, Jr. that ball. . . . I hope it reminds him of who he can be" (Sturm and Tommaso, p. 85).

The sparse prose and stark graphics match the tone and mood of the text well, and the fictional story-within-a-nonfictional story structure helps the reader better appreciate the impact and influence that Satchel Paige had on ordinary African Americans who could not safely and publicly "talk back" to their oppressors. Ultimately, many African Americans lived vicariously through Satchel Paige, who said plenty to white power through his talent and antics on the ball field.

We think graphic novels are a good choice when selecting nonfiction for the secondary ELA classroom. J. Spencer Clark (2012) suggests that understanding "historical agency" requires the ability to "evaluate who was responsible for historical events, as well as to understand the societal factors that either constrained or enabled people's ability to act" (p. 492). Clark suggests graphic novels are good for helping students understand historical agency because they "[expand] the narrative" of the traditional historical story and present "complex relationships and difficult historical situations in which historical actors are faced with external pressures and forced to make choices" (p. 497).

In *Satchel Paige*, we come to understand Emmet, Sr.'s desire to play baseball rather than do back-breaking sharecropping work for 40–50 cents a day, and his desire for his son to go to school rather than join him in the cotton fields. But when Emmet, Sr. is hurt, and Emmet, Jr. is beaten by the Jennings twins, we also come to understand why both of them end up in the fields, working side-by-side. What other options do they have? We also come to understand, ultimately, why Satchel Paige's public shaming of the Jennings twins inspires and empowers both Emmet, Sr., and his son.

Warriors Don't Cry: A Searing Memoir of the Battle to Integrate Little Rock's Central High

In 1957, three years after the United States Supreme Court overturned *Plessy v. Ferguson's* "separate but equal" verdict as unconstitutional in *Brown v. Board of Education* (1954), Melba Pattillo Beals was one of nine African American students (commonly referred to as the "Little Rock Nine") who integrated Central High School in Little Rock, Arkansas. *Warriors Don't Cry* is Beals' memoir, supported with excerpts from her own personal diary, notes from her mother, and newspaper clippings.

Unlike an autobiography, which chronicles the writer's entire life, a memoir focuses on one specific aspect of the writer's life. In her memoir, Beals focuses on her own high school experience, and her attempts to integrate Central High School. As a result, Beals makes readers feel the sting of physical and emotional abuse that the Little Rock Nine suffered as they lived the history of the *Brown v. Board of Education* decision.

In her book *Teaching for Joy and Justice*, Linda Christensen (2009) shares a wonderful unit for teaching Beals' memoir. Christenson explains, "Beals' book tells the story of young people who became accidental heroes when their lives intersected a movement for justice in education, and they made the choice to join the movement instead of taking an easier path" (p. 169). As we learn in the memoir, Beals' choice leads to much heartbreak and hardship for her.

In a 2006 *English Journal* article, Fenice Boyd and Deborah Howe also share a multiple text unit that they taught, centered on *Warriors Don't Cry*, which includes excerpts from the PBS documentary "Eyes on the Prize," the HBO docudrama "Crisis at Central High," and books of photographs. Howe explains that she chose to teach *Warriors Don't Cry* because the book helped her "understand what life under segregation must have felt like more than any other book she had read or taught, including Richard Wright's *Black Boy* and Harper Lee's *To Kill a Mockingbird*" (pp. 61–62).

We think Christensen, Boyd, and Howe provide powerful reasons to include *Warriors Don't Cry* in instruction of TKAM. Ultimately, both the graphic novel of Satchel Paige and Beals' memoir evidence African American resistance to Jim Crow laws, albeit in different ways. As students read these nonfiction texts in conjunction with TKAM, they have opportunities to see that African Americans were not "mere spectators and bystanders in the struggle against their own oppression and exploitation" (Saney, 2003, p. 103), but worked overtly and covertly to speak truth to power and fight for their humanity, dignity, and access to their civil rights.

MANAGING SMALL-GROUP NONFICTION LITERATURE CIRCLES

Defining Good Discussion Skills

As Daniels (2002a, b; 2004) has long suggested, teachers need to put some things in place before sending students off to work in small-group literature circles. For example, teachers should model how literature circles work—using short texts before using whole novels; modeling good questions; and demonstrating the various roles student group members can play. Also central to a successful small-group literature circles activity is that students understand what makes a good discussion. To help our preservice teachers in the methods class consider this and practice the strategy, we modified Daniels' and Steineke's "Defining Discussion Skills" strategy from their 2004 book, *Mini-Lessons for Literature Circles.*

For this strategy, students were given a T-chart with the title "Good Discussion" (see Figure 6.1). The left-hand column was titled "Sounds Like," and the right-hand column was titled "Looks Like." In their first group meeting, students were asked to brainstorm 3–5 skills/statements for each column, based on their own experiences in former class discussions. Group One members listed such skills in the "Sounds Like" column as "take turns speaking" and "respectable questions and answers."

In the second column, Group One members listed the following skills: "turned toward each other"; "looking through the text"; and "all group members are engaged." Group Two members went so far as to list specific statements in the first column, such as: "Great point"; "I like that you . . ."; and "That reminds me of." For the "Looks Like" column, Group Two members listed such skills as "good eye contact"; "one person at a time speaking"; and "equal participation." As we explain later, we asked students to refer to these lists each time they met, and we used these student-created lists in our weekly assessments of the group discussions.

Literature Circle Roles

Before the students met to discuss their books, we explained the nonfiction literature circle roles. Daniels (2002b) explains that literature circle roles can act as "book club training wheels" to help structure the group activity, and goes on to explain the four "basic" roles that can be used to structure the small-group literature discussion. Daniels explains that these roles "reflect fundamental kinds of thinking that real readers habitually use, whether consciously or unconsciously": (1) the connector (connects what students read to their own lives, or to other books, authors, etc.); (2) the questioner (is always wondering about the text); (3) the literary luminary (returns to memorable, important sections in the text); and (4) the illustrator (reminds us that skillful reading requires visualization) (pp. 99–103).

For our instructional purposes (to contextualize the Jim Crow era and highlight the black liberation struggle at the time of Lee's writing), and because we were focusing specifically on the Common Core Reading Standards for Informational Texts, we modified Daniels' roles to include: (1) Summarizer; (2) Interpreter; (3) Crafter and (4) Connector (see Figure 6.2).

Good Discussion...	
Sounds Like	**Looks Like**

Figure 6.1

Students met for literature circles each week during the summer methods course, for 45–60 minutes (they met a total of four times). Students decided how many pages they would read each week at the first meeting, and assigned roles. Roles rotated each week among group members. Instead of coming to meetings prepared with their roles, we told the groups that they could use discussion time to answer the questions for their roles, and that they should collaborate and help each other answer the questions that they were responsible for. Each week students were given a "Due By End of Meeting" sheet that listed our expectations.

Summarizer: What does the text say? (CC Reading/Literacy Standard 2)

Interpreter: What does the text mean? What is the central idea of the text? What seems to be the author's point of view and/or purpose in the text? Be sure to cite textual evidence. (Reading/Literacy Standards 1, 2, 6)

Crafter: How does the text say it? How is the main idea developed over the course of the text? In what order are points made? How are ideas introduced/developed? How does the author tell the story? (Reading/Literacy Standards 2, 3, 5)

As crafter, it might help to consider different types of nonfiction:

§ Narrative nonfiction (storytelling + journalism)
§ Expository (writing to inform)
§ Persuasive (opinionated)
§ Argumentative (evidence-based analysis)
§ Travel writing
§ Memoir/autobiography
§ Biography
§ News story
§ Historical account

As crafter, it might also help to consider different kinds of nonfiction text structures:

§ Cause/Effect
§ Compare/Contrast
§ Pro/Con
§ Problem/Solution
§ Definition/Categorization
§ Order/Sequence/Procedure
§ Description/Listing

Connector: Find or create an account of this topic/story/subject in a different medium to share, and connect both texts (Reading/Literacy Standard 7)

To do this: think about how the nonfiction book connects to *TKAM;* also think about disconnections between *TKAM* and your book--how do the two stories differ? What do you learn in your nonfiction book that you don't learn in *TKAM?* What are some differences between the Black characters and their experiences in *TKAM* and those in your nonfiction text? Also, what other texts (e.g., movies, songs, books, poems, etc.) do you think about when reading TKAM and the nonfiction text?

Figure 6.2

At the end of each class meeting we expected to see: (1) a 4–6 sentence summary of that day's reading; (2) a main idea/textual evidence statement; (3) a craft statement (with example/textual evidence); and (4) a statement about text-to-text connections (between the nonfiction text and TKAM, and also any other text-to-text connections that students made). Each group was given a three-ring binder to hold all of their work. At the front of the binder, we placed their list of "Good Discussion" skills to serve as a reminder, as well as our list of expectations for each week's meeting. We also included a rubric for assessment, which we discuss next.

Assessing Group Discussion

Weekly Assessment

Each week, as the groups met, we walked around and observed the group discussions. As we observed, we took notes in two categories: discussion skills and reading skills (see Figure 6.3). For each group's discussion skills, we used the skills that they had listed on their T-chart at their initial meeting (Figure 6.1). Thus, since Group One listed "turned toward each other" and "all members engaged" in the "Looks Like" column on their T-chart, these were listed as assessment indicators in the discussion skills category on their rubric. As a result, Group One actually lost points for their discussion skills in their first discussion meeting because they were not turned toward each other, but rather, seemed to be working independently on their own individual roles. Thus, all members did not seem engaged with each other. As students realized that we were holding them accountable each week for their discussion skills, we saw much improvement in this area.

In addition to observing discussion skills each week, we also assessed reading skills, as emphasized by the Common Core Reading Standards, including summary-writing skills; ability to state the main idea, using textual evidence; and ability to comment on the structure and style of the text (author craft). Through our weekly assessments (see Figure 6.3), we realized that we needed to introduce strategies to help the students write their weekly summaries, main idea statements, and craft statements. Therefore we introduced the "GIST statement" (Frey, Fisher, and Hernandez, 2003); journalist's questions (Who? What? Where? When? Why? How?) (Urquhart and McIver, 2005); and "Somebody Wanted But So" (Beers, 2003) as summary strategies.

To help students determine the main idea, we explained that the summary should help students get to the main idea, as determining a main idea requires the ability to summarize and predict or infer the author's message. We encouraged students to make predictions about what they thought the authors were trying to achieve, and to choose a word or phrase (textual evidence) they thought described what the text was about.

To help students develop craft statements, we discussed various nonfiction structures (see Figure 6.2) in more detail, and provided some examples. It became obvious to the students, however, that—like Harvey Daniels explains in his article—nonfiction rarely falls neatly into these categories/structures. Talking to Group One about why Sturm and Tommaso might have made the decision to tell Satchel Paige's story through Emmet, Sr.'s eyes—and through a visual medium—proved much more fruitful in helping them think about the structure of the biography and author purpose. Similarly, talking to Group Two about the difference between an autobiography and a memoir, and what part of her life Beals chose to focus on, helped them better understand the choices Beals made in the telling of her story, and her overall purpose for her memoir.

Group #: 1
Meeting #: 1
Book Title: *Striking Out Jim Crow*
Group Members' Names: Karen, Sarah, Carrie, Lynn
Date: June 15
Pages Read This Week: 1-23

Discussion Skills (student-defined)	Group Members					Total Participation?
	Karen	Sarah	Carrie	Lynn		
Take turns speaking	√	√	√	√		yes
Turned toward each other	√	√				no
All members engaged						no
Teacher Comments:	I didn't see much of these "good discussion" skills at work in your group. It looked like you were three working separately on your own roles. Think more about how each of you can contribute to the group.					
Reading Skills	Karen	Sarah	Carrie	Lynn		Total mastery?
Summary	√					no
Main Idea/Textual Evidence		√				no
Structure (Craft)		√				no
Text-to-Text Connections				√		yes
Teacher Comments:	Good work on these skills. We will talk in class about writing good summaries and how to find the main idea. I will also talk to your group about the structure of the graphic novel. Why do you think the authors decided to tell Satchel Paige's story through Emmet, Sr.'s eyes? Good job, Lynn, on the connections to *TKAM*! Keep up the good work group!!					

Figure 6.3

Final Assessment

In her popular book *Assessment Live! 10 Real-Time Ways for Kids to Show What They Know—and Meet the Standards*, Nancy Steineke (2009) explains that assessment should "[put] the students in control and [give] them full responsibility: they take the content they have studied and use it to create something new" (p. 6). Steineke encourages teachers to have students "create" and "perform" assessments because these elucidate what the students—not the teacher—know and can do.

We have used Steineke's "Book Buddy PowerPoint" with students before, and think it makes a good final assessment for small-group literature circle work. We modified this assessment to fit our instructional goals, and asked students to create a minimum 9 slide final PowerPoint presentation that included specific slides (see Figure 6.4), including a slide that elucidated the connections students made between TKAM and the nonfiction text that they read in their small group literature circle. We asked students to think specifically about how the two texts were similar and how they differed, and how the black characters in each text were portrayed. We also asked students to speak in their final presentations about the impact, if any, that the nonfiction text had on shaping their readings and understandings of TKAM, especially in terms of how race relations during the Jim Crow era were depicted in TKAM.

Group One members explained in their final presentation that they appreciated being able to "get inside the head of an African-American character,"

Directions: As you and your group members prepare for the final book presentation you will make to the class, consider the following questions about your book:

- What is the story? What is the main idea?
- Who are the people? Are they heroes?
- What is the structure? How does the author tell this story?
- Where do/does the event(s) take place? Where are we? Why is this important?
- What conflicts, risks, and/or choices are involved?
- What are the value, moral, ethical, and political dimensions of the work?
- What ideas can be debated, disputed?
- What is the "So-What" factor? (Why important? How does it connect to *TKAM*?)

Your group is responsible for putting together an 9-slide (minimum) PowerPoint presentation that includes the following:

1) Book Title/Picture of Book Cover
2) Author Name/Author Photo/Author Bio
3) Summary slide
4) Photos of characters
5) Conflict slide (with photos)
6) Main idea slide (with photos)
7) Graphic that represents text structure
8) Connections to *TKAM*
9) Your group's rating of the book plus three specific reasons for rating

Plan to script your slides and prepare for your portion of the presentation. All members should participate by designing individual slides and presenting individual slides to class.

Figure 6.4

as they did in *Satchel Paige: Striking Out Jim Crow*. Karen, a Group One member, explained that something was missing in TKAM: "You never knew what the Black characters were thinking, but in *Satchel Paige* you did." Lynn, another group member, elaborated on this idea with one of their slides, which included a quotation from *Satchel Paige* where Emmet, Sr. is expressing his frustration about the power relations under Jim Crow: "I thought hard about them Jennings twins, how it came to be that these men lorded over us. How do men so small get so large? Who made it so? You live under their rulin' for so long, you forget who you are, what you can be" (Sturm and Tommaso, p. 83).

Group One members went on to explain that they felt this quotation explained why Emmet, Sr. grows quiet and becomes seemingly obedient in *Satchel Paige* when he has to return to sharecropping after his baseball injury, but then reclaims his humanity and dignity through the larger (and louder)-than-life Satchel Paige. As Lynn explained in her explanation of the group's 4-star rating of the novel, "The ball field where white and Black players met was an equalizer: Black men were able to fight back and challenge white men on the baseball field without getting killed for it."

Group One members went on to point out that Tom Robinson in TKAM—even with Atticus' help—never really has a chance to fight back. To elaborate, Sarah shared a slide with a quotation from TKAM, where Scout is trying to make sense of the jury's guilty verdict: "Atticus had used every tool available to free men to save Tom Robinson, but in the secret courts of men's hearts Atticus had no case. Tom was a dead man the minute Mayella Ewell opened her mouth and screamed" (Lee, p. 244).

Carrie explained that, ultimately, she and her group members felt *Satchel Paige* was "as much about Emmet, Sr.'s catharsis and healing in an oppressive environment as it was about baseball," and furthered that "no such catharsis happens for the Black community in *TKAM*. Only Scout and her family experience any kind of relief and justice." We found these ideas to be particularly insightful.

In addition, Group Two had much to say about *Warriors Don't Cry*. Showing a slide depicting Harper Lee winning the Presidential Medal of Freedom, Daniel explained in his group's final presentation that while Harper Lee is often considered a hero for writing TKAM, Daniel's group felt that Melba Patillo Beals was the true hero, "as she endured physical, emotional, and mental harm on a daily basis to create real change not just for herself, but for others." Daniel's group also questioned the notion that TKAM improved race relations in America, and the more contemporary idea that America is a "post-racial society."

On their last slide, Daniel's group presented Beals' closing words in her memoir: "Today when I see how far we have progressed in terms of school integration . . . I am angry. . . . School integration is still not a reality, and we use children as tender warriors on the battlefield to achieve racial equality" (p. 310). Daniel's group ended their presentation by encouraging the class to think about ways in which racial equality might truly be achieved in public schools.

CONCLUSION

Needless to say, we think the use of the nonfiction texts in conjunction with our reading of TKAM made an important impact on the beginning English teachers in our summer methods course. Not only did many of them say that they were excited to use nonfiction literature circles in their future instruction, but many said that they planned to use the two nonfiction texts we read in class in their own future instruction of TKAM to "provide multiple perspectives" and "get students thinking critically about the time period in which TKAM is set and race relations."

Several students also shared other text-to-text connections that they had made and hoped to use with their class mates, including excerpts from the movies "Remember the Titans" (about integrating a high school football team), and "42" (about Jackie Robinson), and freedom songs (e.g., "We Shall Overcome"). We were excited to hear this, as we realized that the students

Category	Points	Weight	Score
Summary	1 2 3 4 5	X 2	/10
Characters	1 2 3 4 5	X 3	/15
Conflict	1 2 3 4 5	X 2	/10
Structure	1 2 3 4 5	X 2	/10
Main Idea	1 2 3 4 5	X4	/20
Connections	1 2 3 4 5	x3	/15
Passage/Rating	1 2 3 4 5	X2	/10
Presentation Skills (All slides included; professional presentation; evidence of participation from all group members)	1 2 3 4 5	X2	/10
		Total	/100

Figure 6.5

were already thinking about pulling in other black voices and perspectives to teach TKAM. As Kelley (2010) suggests, a "complex" text is one that encourages students to "question, reevaluate, and contextualize a work rather than transform it into something universal and removed from the world in which it was produced, circulated, and read" (p. 12). Appropriately contextualizing *To Kill a Mockingbird* must include representation of the black liberation struggle. With the inclusion of engaging nonfiction that foregrounds the black experience of life and struggle under Jim Crow, we feel confident that ELA teachers can teach TKAM as the exemplary, complex text it is.

REFERENCES

Beals, M. P. (1995). *Warriors Don't Cry: A Searing Memoir of the Battle to Integrate Little Rock's Central High*. New York: Washington Square Press.

Beers, K. (2003). *When Kids Can't Read, What Teachers Can Do: A Guide for Teachers 6-12*. Portsmouth, NH: Heinemann.

Boyd, F. B., and Howe, D. R. (2006). Teaching *Warriors Don't Cry* with other text types to enhance comprehension. *English Journal, 95*(3), 61–68.

Clark, J. S. (2012). Encounters with historical agency: The value of nonfiction graphic novels in the history classroom. *The History Teacher, 46*(4), 489–508.

Christensen, L. (2009). *Teaching for Joy and Justice: Reimagining the Language Arts Classroom*. Milwaukee, WI: Rethinking Schools.

Daniels, H. (2002a). Expository text in literature circles. *Voices from the Middle, 9*(4), 7–14.

Daniels, H. (2002b). *Literature Circles: Voice and Choice in Literature Circles and Reading Groups* (2nd edn). Portland, ME: Stenhouse.

Daniels, H., and Steineke, N. (2004). *Mini-lessons for Literature Circles*. Portsmouth, NH: Heinemann.

Frey, N., Fisher, D., and Hernandez, T. (2003). "What's the gist?" Summary writing for struggling adolescent writers. *Voices in the Middle, 11*(2), 43–49.

Hagberg, L. (2013). Tell me about . . . an informational text that engaged your students: I Have a Dream/*To Kill a Mockingbird*. *Educational Leadership, 17*(3), 90–92.

Kelley, J. B. (2010). What teachers (don't) say: A grounded theory approach to online discussion of *To Kill a Mockingbird*. In M. J. Meyer (Ed.), *Harper Lee's To Kill a Mockingbird: New Essays* (pp. 3–18). Lanham, MD: Scarecrow Press.

Kumler, L., and Palchick, R. (2008). Integrating government and literature: Mock civil and criminal trials based on *To Kill a Mockingbird*. *Social Education, 72*(4), 194–197.

Lee, H. (1962). *To Kill a Mockingbird*. New York: Popular Library.

Maher, S. C. (2013). Using *To Kill a Mockingbird* as a conduit for teaching about the school-to-prison pipeline. *English Journal, 102*(4), 45–52.

National Governors Association Center for Best Practices (2010). "Common Core State Standards." Council of Chief State School Officers, Washington D.C.

Prince William County Public Schools, VA (1997). *To Kill a Mockingbird*: Then & Now—A 35th anniversary celebration. Teacher Study Guide. Retrieved from ERIC database. (ED406711).

Ricker-Wilson, C. (1998). When the mockingbird becomes an albatross: Reading and resistance in the language arts classroom. *English Journal, 87*(3), 67–72.

Saney, I. (2003). The Case Against *To Kill a Mockingbird. Race & Class, 45*(1), 99–110.

Steineke, N. (2009). *Assessment Live! 10 Real-time Ways for Kids to Show What They Know—And Meet the Standards.* Portsmouth, NH: Heinemann.

Sturm, J., and Tommaso, R. (2007). *Satchel Paige: Striking out Jim Crow.* New York: Hyperion Books.

Urquhart, V., and McIver, M. (2005). *Teaching Writing in the Content Areas.* Alexandria, VA: ASCD.

Chapter 7

Graphic Texts as a Catalyst for Content Knowledge and Common Core Content Literacy Standards in Science, Technology, Engineering, and Mathematics Classes

Karina R. Clemmons and Heather A. Olvey

Expressive illustrations in children's literature convey deep meaning and create exceptionally long-lasting memories from our first literary experiences. The powerful melding of image and word is likely due to distinct, but interrelating complex cognitive processes. Researchers in educational psychology suggest that visual input is processed and stored through different processes in the brain from verbal input, but that visual and verbal learning can be connected, and in many instances strengthen one another.

Studies that have investigated the role of images and words in learning and memory indicate that visual processing uses distinct cognitive processes that are different than verbal processing, but that the two processes strengthen one another (Mayer, 2005; Mayer and Anderson, 1992; Miles and Minda, 2011). Multimedia learning that uses words and images concurrently improves learning even when the pictures are static graphic words and pictures are used concurrently (Brannon, 2012; Carter, Hipwell, and Quinnell, 2012; Mayer, 2005). Mayer stated, "People learn more deeply from words and pictures than from words alone" (2005, p. 31).

Graphic novels have evolved alongside illustrated children's literature, comic books, and manga to be officially acclaimed through mainstream awards and to become a growing segment of Young Adult Literature (YAL) (Cole, 2009). Graphic novels have long been considered distinct from comic books in that graphic novels are marketed to young adults, and their content is more complex, often longer, and contains a stand-alone story line rather than a short installment in a more lengthy series (Bucher and Manning, 2004; Weiner, 2003; Yang, 2008).

While many authors consider graphic novels as a genre (Bucher and Manning, 2004; Clark, 2013; Connors, 2013; Kaplan, 2012; Hoover, 2012;

Figure 7.1 The power of images. Karina R. Clemmons. *Source*: This comic strip was generated at http://www.MakeBeliefsComix.com. Used with permission of author and site creator Bill Zimmerman.

Yang, 2008), others increasingly distinguish graphic novels as a category, format, medium, or form (Behler, 2006; Chute, 2008; Chute and DeKoven, 2006; Cole, 2009; Fletcher-Spear, Jenson-Benjamin, and Copeland, 2005; Gonzalez, 2014; Ward, Young, and Day, 2012). To complicate these distinctions in classification, it should be noted that the current definition of "genre" includes literary variations of style and form (Merriam-Webster, n.d.).

These distinctions in terminology are germane to a discussion of implications for the acceptance, perceived relevance, and even access to literature in graphic form. For example, a librarian responsible for all youth literature acquisitions for a metropolitan library system noted that she initiated a change in the cataloging system to place a "graphic" designation on graphic novels and to shelve them together as a format (A. Miller, email communication, June 12, 2014). Additionally, changes in the call number system for fiction graphic novels use a series title so that books in a series are shelved together regardless of author.

These two changes allow readers to search for and find graphic novels more readily. Miller notes, however, that nonfiction categorization remains a challenge as the current cataloging protocol does not allow for a graphic *novel* to be nonfiction. The cataloging protocol neither assigns a graphic designation nor shelves graphic nonfiction together as a category; thus nonfiction graphic texts are simply cataloged with the Dewey decimal system by topic. While shelving nonfiction graphic texts without a "graphic" designation serves to legitimize graphic texts as accepted nonfiction sources, this also makes the format more difficult for readers and teachers to find (A. Miller, email communication, June 12, 2014).

Fletcher-Spear, Jenson-Benjamin, and Copeland (2005) stated, "Instead of thinking of them as a genre, it is necessary to think of them as a format" (p. 37). Gonzalez (2014) agrees that "viewing graphic novels as an isolate genre is detrimental to integrating graphic novels throughout the whole curriculum" (p. 3), as graphic novels can be of any genre and cover a wide range of topics. After careful consideration, the authors have concurred, and will refer to graphic texts as a format in this chapter.

One thing is clear; students are drawn to the illustrative story telling in graphic novels, which make them an excellent instructional resource (Behler, 2006; Short and Reeves, 2009; Yang, 2008). Though previously thought to be most useful in academic settings for reluctant readers, boys, English learners, and hearing impaired students (Behler, 2006; Fletcher-Spear, Jenson-Benjamin, and Copeland, 2005; Smetana et al., 2009; Temple, 2009; Yang, 2008), it has become clear that graphic novels are complex, multifaceted, and have far-reaching interest to diverse adolescents (Brannon, 2012; Connors, 2013; Jaffe, 2013).

Thus graphic novels have become increasingly recognized as resources in middle school and high school classes (Behler, 2006; Clark, 2013; Griffith, 2010; Hoover, 2012; Monnin, 2013). Clark (2013) noted that "graphic novels are recognized as valuable resources in multiple subject areas for their engaging qualities and use of multiple perspectives" (p. 490).

NO LONGER ONLY GRAPHIC "NOVELS": RICH NONFICTION CONTRIBUTIONS

Currently, graphic literature has grown so rich that the term "graphic novel" has become in many cases a misnomer, as the word "novel" presumes fiction, but the graphic format now contains substantial nonfiction contributions as well (Chute, 2006; Clark, 2013; Ward, Young, and Day, 2012). To reconcile the nomenclature to this growing diversity, current literature contains the term "graphic literature" (Martin, 2009), "graphic narrative" (Chute, 2008), and "non-fiction graphic novel" (Clark, 2013) alongside the frequently used term "graphic novel" (Behler, 2006; Cole, 2009; Griffith, 2010; Hoover, 2012; Monnin, 2013; Yang, 2008). The authors clarify this confusion by referring to all YAL in graphic format as "graphic texts," which may contain fiction and nonfiction in any genre.

After a thorough review of current YAL graphic texts with relevancy for science, technology, engineering, and math (STEM) fields, the authors identified three categories that are pertinent to any future discussion of YAL's relevance in STEM classes: graphic novels with nonfiction themes, graphic nonfiction narratives, and graphic informational texts. It is especially important to distinguish among these categories so that STEM educators are aware of the amount of fictionalization, if any, of different YAL graphic texts and can plan content and literacy activities accordingly.

A "graphic novel with non-fiction themes" describes works of majority fiction that contain substantial themes of nonfiction topics. For example, *Space Race: A Graphic Novel* (Walsh and Jones, 2011) is best categorized as a graphic novel with nonfiction themes. This YAL text contains historical information about the history of space exploration, rocket engineering, and the space race. The nonfiction content is framed within a science fiction setting in which a boy and his grandfather discuss controversial events that they experience in their futuristic world while on a fishing trip.

Graphic novels with nonfiction themes are primarily works of fiction, and are thus not intended to serve primarily as factual resources. Graphic novels with strong nonfiction themes are an excellent resource to gain student interest in a topic or instructional unit in STEM classes, and are well suited for activities that generate student discussion, analysis, and research of fact versus fiction on a given topic after reading the YAL graphic text.

A "graphic non-fiction narrative" is a work of majority nonfiction that is told in narrative form, occasionally filling in with fiction in order to maintain the narrative quality of the graphic text. Ottaviani and Wicks' 2013 graphic text *Primates: The Fearless Science of Jane Goodall, Dian Fossey, and Biruté Galdikas* would fall into this category. The text is almost exclusively based on facts about the lives and the research of the three famous primatologists, and is grounded in published research, autobiographies, print and video interviews, and other written correspondence.

The authors acknowledge that a narrative form guides this YAL graphic text, and occasional liberties are taken in order to serve the narrative and connect the reader to the personal experiences of the scientists' lives and contributions to the field of primatology.

Graphic nonfiction narratives are an excellent resource to draw adolescents into reading about the human side of important lives, scientific method, and pivotal discoveries. Using graphic nonfiction narratives in STEM classes offers teachers a chance to build the relevance of STEM topics from a more personal perspective. In addition, graphic nonfiction narratives can include developing students' critical reading and thinking skills with activities that call upon students to analyze and add to the YAL texts with their own information from other sources.

"Graphic informational texts" are distinct from traditional textbooks that contain some graphics (e.g., illustrations, photos, charts, diagrams) interspersed among primarily objective informational text. Graphic informational texts also contain a wealth of objective informational content, but are marketed to young adults through the primary use of visually appealing and thought-provoking illustrations with limited text. What sets graphic informational texts apart from textbooks is that the method of information delivery is primarily graphics intended to convey as much conceptual information as possible with concise wording.

These YAL texts may also contain personalizing humor interspersed with explanations of seemingly difficult concepts. The humor frequently takes the form of a narrator who speaks directly to the reader about the concepts; or in some cases, a narrator who speaks to other characters within the graphic text. Graphic informational texts such as *Charles Darwin's* On the Origin of the Species*: A Graphic Adaptation* (Keller and Fuller, 2009), *Wonderful Life with the Elements* (Yorifuji, 2012), and *Cartoon Introduction to Economics Volume One: Microeconomics* (Bauman and Klein, 2010) are well suited to engage adolescent readers in vast amounts of content in an accessible and visually appealing format.

The authors assert that in order to best use graphic texts in STEM classes with a purpose, it is vital that educators recognize the aforementioned categories of graphic texts and their varying proportions of nonfiction to fiction, and use this knowledge to plan class activities and student analysis accordingly.

CONTENT AND LITERACY IN STEM CLASSES: COMPATIBLE, NOT COMPETING

The Next Generation Science Standards (National Research Council, 2012b) have established essential learning practices for K–12 students that are based on the National Research Council's (2012a) recommendations of the Framework for K–12 Science Education. The Next Generation Science Standards (NGSS, 2012b) include critical thinking skills such as asking and defining problems; analyzing and interpreting data; constructing explanations and designing solutions; engaging in argument from evidence; and obtaining, evaluating, and communicating information. NGSS challenge teachers to alter traditional instruction to encourage students to actively develop knowledge through critical thinking rather than simply completing pre-designed, step-by-step lessons and labs (Robelen, 2013).

Like the NGSS, the Common Core State Standards (CCSS) for math also indicate increased expectations in components of critical thinking, specifically focus, coherence, and rigor ("Key Shifts," 2014). For example, the standard that requires students to have the ability to "look for and express regularity in repeated reasoning" (CCSS, 2012) demonstrates the shift of the new standards to expect and operationalize critical thinking in math. Adopted by the vast majority of the states, the CCSS for math call for an equal focus on "conceptual understanding, procedural skills and fluency, and application" ("Key Shifts," 2014).

The CCSS for literacy in core content classes also represent a paradigm shift that declares that literacy skills such as reading, discussing, and analyzing are vital for student success in *all* academic classes, not only in English language arts (ELA) classes. CCSS require that basic literacy in all content classes includes building strong content knowledge through comprehension, evaluating evidence, critiquing, and reading a variety of literary and informational texts (CCSS, 2012). With CCSS for literacy, students are expected to cite textual evidence to support analysis of texts; determine central ideas, summaries, and conclusions; determine the meaning of domain-specific vocabulary used in technical contexts; identify important unresolved issues in a text; integrate, evaluate, and synthesize information from diverse sources.

Carter (2013) noted that the ability to derive meaning from visuals of many forms (e.g., pictures, diagrams, charts, graphs) is an essential skill for students in all STEM classes. She suggests that teachers should actively seek to help students develop visual literacy, or the ability to decode and encode visual information.

Additionally, a sampling of CCSS for mathematical practice connects content and literacy (CCSS, 2012), indicating that in addition to procedural fluency in mathematical skills, students should be able to make sense of written problems and persevere in solving them; read the arguments of others and decide whether they make sense; ask useful questions to clarify and improve arguments; construct arguments and critique the reasoning of others; justify and communicate conclusions to others; and examine claims and make explicit use of definitions, terminology, logic, and reasoning for support.

Facing a landscape of complex new standards, STEM teachers need instructional resources to help seamlessly integrate content and literacy. Though graphic texts have been recognized as valuable instructional resources in ELA and content classes (Brannon, 2012; Bucher and Manning, 2004; Clark, 2013; Griffith, 2010; Martin, 2009), an extensive literature review indicates there has been little attention to the use of YAL graphic texts in STEM classes. With ever-increasing nonfiction contributions of YAL in a graphic format, graphic texts are poised to engage students in content and literacy in STEM classes. The instructional resources that follow illustrate how content and literacy meaningfully merge through activities with YAL graphic texts that are relevant to STEM fields.

YAL GRAPHIC TEXTS IN ACTION IN STEM CLASSES

The three YAL graphic texts in this chapter were specifically chosen because the texts offer recent content coverage relevant to all STEM fields. Furthermore, each graphic text is representative of one of the three categories discussed in depth in the chapter: graphic novels with nonfiction themes, graphic nonfiction narrative, and graphic informational text. In addition to the detailed instructional activities, a complete resource list of recent YAL graphic texts, their corresponding graphic text categories, and the STEM concepts contained within each text can be found in Figure 7.2.

Preparing for the Graphic Format

Authors have noted that graphic texts are distinct from prose novels in their visual format and thus require a brief instruction for how to best read them (Fletcher-Spear, Jenson-Benjamin, and Copeland, 2005; Gonzalez, 2014). Readers should recognize that pictures and words work together to tell a story in graphic texts. McCloud's 1993 book *Understanding Comics* delves into this theme in depth. In the book, McCloud states, "Words, pictures, and other icons are the vocabulary of the language called comics" (1993, p. 47). Brief instruction on how to read graphic texts will help students create meaning from the graphic format and also serve to facilitate classroom conversations of the YAL texts.

Regarding visuals, basic information includes knowledge that the squares that contain the illustrations are called panels and the spaces between panels are called gutters. The gutters signify what happens between the panels, and for the story to work, it takes the reader's own critical thinking inferences to picture how things happen there.

Panels are generally read from left to right, and top to bottom; however, artists can vary the sequence in the way they draw the panels. For example, panels don't always have to be the same size, and they don't always have to be rectangles.

If the page does not follow the typical order, it is the artist's job to make sure that the size and order of the panels lead the reader's eye in the correct path. This can be done by overlapping panels in a certain way, or even by using "bleeds," which are panels that, rather than being encapsulated, run off the end of the page (McCloud, 1993), giving more presence and importance to that panel.

The concise words contained in the panels are often formatted for varying purposes. Some of the words in the panels are used to indicate background information. Thought balloons and speech bubbles are formatted specifically to convey thoughts, spoken words, or even sounds. Pictures in graphic texts are also intended to convey a great deal of information, so readers should devote attention to interpreting the pictures that tell much of the story.

The concept of closure, in which the reader's inferences between frames are vital, is integral to the development of graphic texts. McCloud defines closure as the "phenomenon of observing the parts but perceiving the whole" (1993, p. 63). In other words, the reader's mind has to finish what the panels start. A static picture can only show so much motion and/or time, so that as the reader moves from panel to panel, he or she finishes the action based on experience of how similar things happen in life.

"Comic panels fracture both time and space offering a jagged, staccato rhythm of unconnected moments. But closure allows us to connect these moments" (McCloud, 1993, p. 67). For this reason, readers of graphic texts must be active participants in order to keep the story moving; reading passively will not work to fully understand, appreciate, and enjoy this medium.

Logicomix: An Epic Search for Truth

This YAL graphic narrative with nonfiction themes by Doxiadis, Papadimitriou, Papadatos, and Di Donna (2009) is an engaging YAL resource for math teachers. The authors and illustrators are characters in the book, and through their discussions of logic and the search for truth, they tell the story of Bertrand Russell's life and his pursuit of logical mathematical absolutes. The illustrations are vivid and will capture readers' attention, and the content touches upon so many subjects that diverse adolescents should find something in the book that interests them. Sections of this book could be used in grades 9 and 10, but because of the complexity of the subjects and the length of the book, it is recommended as a complete text in grades 11–12. Standards covered:

- CCSS Math Practice 3: Construct viable arguments and critique the reasoning of others
- CCSS Math Practices 8: Look for and express regularity in repeated meaning
- CCSS RL.11–12.2: Determine two or more themes or central ideas of a text and analyze their development over the course of the text, including how they interact and build on one another to produce a complex account; provide an objective summary of the text
- CCSS RI.11–12.10: Read and comprehend complex literary and informational texts independently and proficiently

Activity 1: Looking for Logic and Repeated Meaning

After students read the first section of the book through page 73, teach logic concepts. Logic puzzles offer a great segue into geometric proofs by offering the needed skills in a simulation of a real-world situation (P. Chmielewski, personal communication, July 2014). Have students go to http://www.

logic-puzzles.org/, and discuss what logic puzzles are and how to solve them by using the site's explanation as a guide. This site offers the ability to customize both the difficulty level, as well as the size of the grid, so students can begin individually by solving a less challenging puzzle on the smallest grid. Once students have had success solving a puzzle on their own, they can be divided into groups to solve a more difficult puzzle. After the students have grappled with the puzzles in groups, the teacher can then transition to the teaching of geometric proofs.

Activity 2: Summarizing Important Points

After reading the book, divide students into groups and direct them to "The Notebook" at the end of the text. Assign each group a specific number of entries, and have them pull out the important points for the theories or people for which they are responsible. Each group should fill out a chart with the pertinent information that they will then share with the other groups so that all students will have a complete chart that will help them prepare for their assessment.

Activity 3: Correlating with an Outside Informational Text

Give students a copy of Bertrand Russell's essay entitled "The Study of Mathematics" (found at gutenburg.com), and have them read and annotate the essay individually. Break students into groups to discuss and summarize the text, and assign each group to list some "effects of mathematics upon practical life" that Russell discusses, both mentioning the ones he specifically lists, as well as adding some that are more applicable to life today. Then ask the groups to prepare for a debate regarding the merit of mathematics in today's world. For advanced learners, have them develop their own topics to debate based upon Russell's essay.

Assessment

Instruct students to visit Gene Yang's website http://geneyang.com/factoring/, to see what informational text in a graphic format looks like. Have students summarize the important points of *Logicomix* by creating their own informational comic strips. They can either draw it out by hand, or use a website such as http://www.MakeBeliefsComix.com. Students should include Russell's major works and theories, as well as some of the players who had an impact on Russell.

Trinity: A Graphic History of the First Atomic Bomb

This YAL graphic nonfiction narrative by Fetter-Vorm (2012) is an excellent resource for science, technology, and engineering classrooms. Though primarily informative on the history of the atomic bomb and its scientific, political, and historical background, the graphic text contains threads of fictional narrative elements that personalize the statistics of war. The illustrations are black and white, but the ethical dilemmas that this graphic novel introduces are anything but simple. The illustrated discussion of some of the more graphic effects of the atomic bomb leave this novel best suited for grades 9–12. Standards covered:

- NGSS 4: Analyze and interpret data
- NGSS 8: Obtain, evaluate, and communicate information
- CCSS 2: Determine the central ideas or conclusions of a text; summarize complex concepts, processes, or information presented in a text by paraphrasing them in simpler but still accurate terms
- CCSS 8: Evaluate the hypothesis, data, analysis, and conclusions in a scientific text, verifying the data when possible and corroborating or challenging conclusions from other sources of information.

Activity 1: Summarize Complex Concepts and Processes

After students read the first third of the book through page 59, assign students to groups. Each group should collaboratively review the text through page 59, and then create a poster or multimedia bulletin board using padlet.com that describes the distinct scientific principles behind the bombs nicknamed "Little Boy" and "Fat Man." Let the students think in what ways the designs differ in terms of design and scientific process? Then instruct them to create a concise list of influential scientific discoveries and their corresponding contextual backgrounds (e.g., scientist, culture, time frame, cultural reception).

Activity 2: Generating Questions and Defining Problems

After finishing the YAL graphic novel, assign students to groups to generate a list of scientific and ethical questions that are left unanswered in the text. Group members should collaborate to decide on the most pressing questions, and then brainstorm possible sources of information for research for those questions. The group should collaboratively investigate various reputable sources on their topics and report back to the class. Class members should be active listeners by taking notes on questions that they have on the topic to generate further discussion.

Activity 3: Evaluating Data and Sources

Review the author's list of sources included in the appendix of the book. Divide the class into work groups, assigning each group to collaboratively locate, read, analyze and report on one assigned original source from the appendix. How closely did the author rely on the original source? What variations and interpretations of the original source were noted when the original source was compared to the author's narration of the same process or events? Why might the author have chosen to include and omit specific information in the graphic novel? After each group reports their analysis of the original source and the author's description in the graphic text, discuss the implications as a class. How does reading the original source material impact the readers' evaluations of the accuracy of the information presented in the text? What further questions remain?

Assessment

After reading the book and discussing it in class, break students into groups and give them one class period to prepare a lesson that they will have to teach the entire class the next day. One group can be tasked with explaining what nuclear fission is and how it works; another can be in charge of explaining what a chain reaction is; and a different group can be responsible for the major players in the creation of the atomic bomb and each person's scientific contribution. Students should include visuals in their explanations, and use props if it would be helpful. If there is access to a computer lab, students can prepare a Prezi or PowerPoint to aid in their lesson. After all the presentations, students may demonstrate knowledge of all the important concepts with a brief quiz.

Charles Darwin's On the Origin of the Species: *A Graphic Adaptation*

This YAL graphic informational text by Keller and Fuller (2009) is an excellent resource for science teachers who want to engage students in the pioneering research of Charles Darwin. Through dialogue and vivid illustrations, this YAL graphic text explores the historical and controversial background of Darwin's work that forever changed science and perceptions, and would best be suited for grades 7–12. Standards covered:

- NGSS 1: Ask questions and define problems
- NGSS 8: Obtain, evaluate, and communicate information
- CCSS 1: Cite specific textual evidence to support analysis of science and technical texts, attending to important distinctions that the author makes and to any gap or inconsistencies in the account
- CCSS 6: Analyze the author's purpose in providing an explanation, describing a procedure, or discussing an experiment in a text, identifying important issues that remain unsolved

Activity 1: Examine Motivation, Questions, and Scientific Process

Before reading "Part I: Beginnings of a Theory," guide students through a graphic organizer pre-reading strategy. Direct students to draw lines to divide a piece of notebook paper into three equal columns. Label the first column "Motivation," the second column "Guiding Questions," and the third column "Scientific Process and Evidence." As students read the chapter, they should take notes under each column heading as they learn more about Darwin and his theory.

Create a large classroom chart with the same headings as listed above. Call on students to contribute notes to the classroom chart. Use this collaborative chart to spur a class discussion of the personal, social, and historical context of Darwin's work, as well as the method through which Darwin began his investigations. Compare Darwin's methods of investigation to current expectations for scientific method. What similarities and what differences exist? How might modern scientists investigate similar questions?

Activity 2: Investigate and Report on Specialized Adaptations

After reading chapter 6 "Examples of Specialized Adaptations," review the information as a class. After the class discussion, assign students to groups in which they research other animals with specialized adaptations. Students should work to create a short presentation that would contain information about the animals researched and their adaptations for eating, reproducing, and defense. Each presentation should contain visual aids prepared in presentation software such as prezi.com or PowerPoint to illustrate the results of the research and the sources of information.

To practice active listening and note-taking skills, students who are listening to each group's presentation should take notes on each animal presented for use in the following post-presentation activity and suggest additional creative adaptations that could help the animals identified.

Activity 3: Analysis and Extension to Develop Meaning

In addition to narrative illustrations in chapter 15 "Recapitulation and Conclusion," there are seven excerpts from Darwin's writings that are quoted in the chapter. Assign students to work together in pairs to first analyze each excerpt for meaning, and then rewrite each excerpt in modern language. Use a jigsaw instructional technique to share the rewrites by choosing one excerpt from each group to share. After students read the timeline in the Afterword, have them consider the events after the publication of Darwin's *On the Origin of Species* in 1859. The timeline in the Afterword contains events to 2006. Instruct students to research and add more recent scientific research and discoveries that have further developed concepts described in the book.

Assessment

After reading the book, revisit the map of the travels of the Beagle in "Part Beginning of a Theory." To assess knowledge and comprehension of the content, have students summarize and discuss Darwin's observations in several diverse geographic areas of his travels. For further analysis, evaluation, and synthesis, offer students choices of other geographic areas that Darwin did not visit, such as the Aleutian Islands, the central US Plains, or the Yucatan Peninsula.

Require students to consider examples of local fauna and discuss examples of variation, survival of the fittest, instinct, and geographical distribution. Modifications: Include a word bank to accommodate learners with special needs. Offer students different options to show their knowledge of content concepts, such as through sketches, diagrams, and bulleted lists.

YAL GRAPHIC TEXTS AS VALUABLE RESOURCES FOR STEM CLASSES

The National Science Education Standards (National Research Council, 1996), the Principles and Standards for School Mathematics (National Council of Teachers of Mathematics, NCTM, 2000), and the CCSS (2012) all emphasize the essential nature of preparing students for literacy and to think critically. CCSS challenge educators to help students "demonstrate independence, build strong content knowledge," and "value evidence" (CCSS, 2012).

Several key components of the NCTM's Process Standards (2011) are building new mathematical knowledge through problem solving and applying a variety of strategies to solve problems. A new National Science Teachers Association conceptual framework highlights the need to prepare students to approach science as active self-motivated investigation (NSTA, 2012), calling for students to develop, plan, analyze, adapt, and evaluate self-directed investigations (Reisner, Berland, and Kenyon, 2012).

Connors (2013) asserted, "Textual complexity is not the sole reserve of the classics" (p. 69). Smetana, Odelson, Burns, and Grisham (2009) also indicated, "The skills students use to interpret graphic novels include analysis, interpretation, and conjecture, all higher order thinking skills" (p. 230). Teachers in STEM classes can build on adolescents' attraction to graphic novels in order to increase student engagement, build on content knowledge, teach interpretation of visuals, and approach CCSS literacy standards.

In conclusion, new standards in STEM fields and new literacy standards for all core classes require students to proficiently comprehend and digest text and content simultaneously. NGSS and CCSS do not compete; rather, the new standards recognize that content knowledge and literacy go hand in

Title	Author/Illustrator	Year	Category	STEM Field: Themes
The Cartoon Introduction to Economics Volume One: Microeconomics	Yoram Baumann/ Grady Klein	2010	Graphic Informational Text	Math: Economics
The Cartoon Introduction to Economics Volume Two: Macroeconomics	Yoram Baumann/ Grady Klein	2011	Graphic Informational Text	Math: Economics
Charles Darwin's On the Origin of the Species: A Graphic Adaptation	Michael Keller/ Nicole Rager Fuller	2009	Graphic Informational Text	Science: Darwin's theory of evolution
The Inventor: The Story of Tesla	Rave Mehta/ Erik Williams	2014	Graphic Non-Fiction Narrative	Science, Technology: Tesla's inventions
Levitation: Physics and Psychology in the Service of Deception	Jim Ottaviani/ Janine Johnston	2007	Graphic Novel with Non-Fiction Themes	Science: Physics, perception and magic
Logicomix: An Epic Search for Truth	Apostolos Doxiadis, Christos H. Papadimitriou/ Alecos Papadatos, Annie Di Donna	2009	Graphic Novel with Non-Fiction Themes	Math: Life of Bertrand Russell, logic, religion, philosophy
The Manga Guide to Calculus	Hiroyuki Kojima, Shin Togam/	2009	Graphic Novel with Non-Fiction Themes	Math: Calculus
The Manga Guide to Electricity	Kazuhiro Fujitaki/Iroha Inoue	2009	Graphic Novel with Non-Fiction Themes	Science: Electricity
The Manga Guide to Linear Algebra	Shin Taka/ Iroha Inoue	2012	Graphic Novel with Non-Fiction Themes	Math: Algebra
The Manga Guide to Physics	Hideo Nitta/ Keita Takatsu	2009	Graphic Novel with Non-Fiction Themes	Science: Physics
Primates: The Fearless Science of Jane Goodall, Dian Fossey, and Biruté Galdikas	Jim Ottaviani/ Maris Wicks	2013	Graphic Non-Fiction Narrative	Science: Goodall, Fossey, and Galdikas' lives and contributions to the study of primates
Space Race: A Graphic Novel	CEL Walsh/ K. L. Jones	2011	Graphic Novel with Non-Fiction Themes	Engineering, Technology, Science: History of the space race, rockets, space shuttles
The Stuff of Life: A Graphic Guide to Genetics and DNA	Mark Shultz/ Zander Cannon, Kevin Cannon	2009	Graphic Novel with Non-Fiction Themes	Science: Biology, genetics, DNA
T-Minus: The Race to the Moon	Jim Ottaviani/ Zander Cannon, Kevin Cannon	2009	Graphic Non-Fiction Narrative	Engineering, Technology, Science: History of the race to the moon
Trinity: A Graphic History of the First Atomic Bomb	Jonathan Fetter-Vorm	2013	Graphic Non-Fiction Narrative	Engineering, Technology: Physics, nuclear physics, history of atomic bomb
Wonderful Life with the Elements	Bunpei Yorifuji	2012	Graphic Informational Text	Science: Chemistry, elements, periodic table

Figure 7.2   Appendix A: Release for Use of Introductory Graphic

hand to build depth of knowledge and the ability to evaluate and synthesize. Graphic YAL texts such as those discussed in depth in this chapter offer a powerful resource for educators to seamlessly integrate content, literacy, and critical thinking to prepare students for success in the twenty-first century.

REFERENCES

Bauman, Y., and Klein, G. (2010). *The Cartoon Introduction to Economics: Volume One: Microeconomics.* New York, NY: Hill and Wang.

Behler, A. (2006). Getting started with graphic novels: A guide for the beginner. *The Alert Collector: Reference & User Services Quarterly, 46*(2), 16–21.

Brannon, A. (2012). Translation, not adaptation: Reading Gareth Hind's graphic *Odyssey. SIGNAL, 35*(2), 38–43.

Bucher, K. T., and Manning, L. M. (2004). Bringing graphic novels into a school's curriculum. *The Clearing House, 78*(2), 67–72.

Carter, M. G. (2013). A picture is worth a thousand words: A cross-curricular approach to learning about visuals in STEM. *2nd International STEM in Education Conference.* Retrieved from http://stem2012.bnu.edu.cn/data/long%20paper/stem2012_26.pdf.

Carter, M. G., Hipwell, P., and Quinnell, L. (2012). A picture is worth a thousand words: An approach to learning about visuals. *Australian Journal of Middle Schooling, 12*(2), 5–15.

Chute, H. (2008). Comics as literature? Reading graphic narrative. *PMLA, 123*(2), 452–65. Retrieved from http://people.uncw.edu/jualls/420_comics_as_literature.pdf.

Chute, H. L., and DeKoven, M. (2006). Introduction: Graphic narratives. *MFS Modern Fiction Studies, 52*(4), 767–82. Retrieved from http://0-muse.jhu.edu.iii-server.ualr.edu/journals/modern_fiction_studies/v052/52.4chute01.pdf.

Clark, J. S. (2013). Encounters with historical agency: The value of nonfiction graphic novels in the classroom. *The History Teacher, 46*(4), 489–508. Retrieved from http://www.societyforhistoryeducation.org/pdfs/A13_Clark.pdf.

Cole, P. (2009). *Young Adult Literature in the 21st Century.* New York, NY: McGraw Hill.

Common Core State Standards (2012). Common Core State Standards for English language arts & literacy in history/social studies, science, and technical subjects. Retrieved from http://www.corestandards.org/.

Connors, S. P. (2013). Challenging perspectives on young adult literature. *English Journal, 102*(5), 69–73.

Doxiadis, A., Papadimitriou, H., Papadatos, A., and Di Donna, A. (2009). *Logicomix: An Epic Search for Truth.* New York, NY: Bloomsbury.

Fetter-Vorm, J. (2013). *Trinity: A Graphic History of the First Atomic Bomb.* New York, NY: Hill and Wang.

Fletcher-Spear, K., Jenson-Benjamin, M., and Copeland, T. (2005). The truth about graphic novels: A format, not a genre. *ALAN Review, 32*(2), 37–44.

Genre. (n.d.). *Merriam-Webster Online Dictionary.* Retrieved from http://www.merriam-webster.com/dictionary/genre.

Gonzalez, A. (2014). It's more than just a comic! An introduction to the graphic novel. *Adolescent Literacy in Perspective.* Retrieved from http://ohiorc.org/orc_documents/ORC/Adlit/InPerspective/2014-02/in_perspective_2014-02.pdf.

Griffith, P. E. (2010). Graphic novels in the secondary classroom and school libraries. *Journal of Adolescent & Adult Literacy, 54*(3), 181–89.

Hoover, S. (2012). The case for graphic novels. *Communications in Information Literacy, 5*(2), 174–86.

Jaffe, M. (2013). Raising a reader! How comics and graphic novels can help your kids love to read. *A Comic Book Legal Defense Fund Publication.* Retrieved from http://cbldf.org/resources/raising-a-reader/.

Kaplan, J. S. (2012). The changing face of young adult literature: What teachers and researchers need to know to enhance their practice and inquiry. In J. A. Hayn and J. S. Kaplan (Eds.), *Teaching Young Adult Literature Today* (pp. 19–40). Lanham, MD: Rowman & Littlefield Publishers, Inc.

Keller, M., and Fuller, N. R. (2009). *Charles Darwin's* On the Origin of the Species: *A Graphic Adaptation.* Emmaus, PA: Rodale Books.

Key shifts in mathematics (2014). Common Core State Standards Initiative. Retrieved from http://www.corestandards.org/other-resources/key-shifts-in-mathematics/.

Martin, A. (2009). Graphic novels in the classroom. *Library Media Connection, 28,* 30–31.

Mayer, R. E. (2005). Cognitive theory of multimedia learning. In R. E. Mayer (Ed.), *Handbook of Multimedia Learning* (pp. 31–48). Cambridge, England: Cambridge University Press.

Mayer, R. E., and Anderson, R. B. (1992). The instructive animation: Helping students build connections between words and pictures in multimedia learning. *Journal of Educational Psychology, 84*(4), 444–52.

McCloud, S. (1993). *Understanding Comics: The Invisible Art.* New York, NY: Harper Perennial.

Miles, S. J., and Minda, J. P. (2011). The effects of concurrent verbal and visual tasks on category learning. *Journal of Experimental Psychology, 37*(3), 588–607. doi:10.1037/a0022309.

Monnin, J. (2013). Aligning graphic novels to the common core standards. *Knowledge Quest, 41*(3), 50–56.

National Council of Teachers of Mathematics (2000). *Principles and Standards for School Mathematics.* Reston, VA: NCTM.

National Council of Teachers of Mathematics (2011). *Process Standards.* Retrieved from http://www.nctm.org/standards/content.aspx?id=322.

National Research Council (1996). *National Science Education Standards.* Washington, DC: National Academies Press.

National Research Council (2012a). *A Framework for K-12 Science Education: Practices, Cross-cutting Concepts, and Core Ideas.* Washington, DC: National Academies Press.

National Research Council (2012b). *Next Generation Science Standards: New Standards for a New Generation.* Washington, DC: National Academies Press. Retrieved from http://www.nextgenscience.org/.

National Science Teachers Association (2012). *Framework for K-12 Science Education.* Retrieved from http://www.nsta.org/about/standardsupdate/resources.aspx.

Ottaviani, J., and Wicks, M. (2013). *Primates: The Fearless Science of Jane Goodall, Dian Fossey, and Biruté Galdikas.* New York, NY: First Second.

Reisner, B. J., Berland, L. K., and Kenyon, L. (2012). Engaging students in the scientific practices of explanation and argumentation: Understanding a framework for K-12 science education. *Science and Children,* April/May 2012, 8–13.

Robelen, E. W. (2013). Teachers shift instructional approaches to bring "next generation" into class. *Education Week, 32*(31), 1–13.

Short, J. C., and Reeves, T. C. (2009). The graphic novel: A "cool" format for communicating to Generation Y. *Business Communication Quarterly, 72*(4), 414–30.

Smetana, L., Odelson, D., Burns, H., and Grisham, D. L. (2009). Using graphic novels in the high school classroom: Engaging deaf students with a new genre. *Journal of Adolescent & Adult Literacy, 53*(3), 228–40.

Temple, B. (2009). Graphic novels in the ESL classroom. *Humanising Language Teaching.* Retrieved from http://www.hltmag.co.uk/jun09/mart03.htm#top.

Walsh, C. E. L., and Jones, K. L. (2011). *Space Race: A Graphic Novel.* New York, NY: Campfire.

Ward, B. A., Young, T. A., and Day, D. (2012). Crossing boundaries: Genre-blurring in books for young adults. In J. A. Hayn and J. S. Kaplan (Eds.), *Teaching Young Adult Literature Today* (pp. 167–83). Lanham, MD: Rowman & Littlefield Publishers, Inc.

Weiner, S. (2003). *Faster than a Speeding Bullet: The Rise of the Graphic Novel* (2nd ed.). New York, NY: Nantier, Beall, Minoustchine Publishing Inc.

Yang, G. (2008). Graphic novels in the classroom. *Language Arts, 85*(3), 185–92.

Yorifuji, B. (2012). *Wonderful Life with the Elements: The Periodic Table Personified.* San Francisco, CA: No Starch Press, Inc.

Chapter 8

Annotated Resources for the Classroom Teacher

Judith A. Hayn, Kent Layton, and Heather A. Olvey

It is well known that the Common Core State Standards (CCSS) call for literacy to be taught across the content areas, meaning that students must become adept at reading and writing in all of their subject areas. Yet, Shanahan and Shanahan (2012) argue in their article "What is Disciplinary Literacy and Why does it Matter?" that content area literacy is insufficient to meet the close reading needs required by CCSS.

While content area reading acknowledges that there are differences among the different disciplines, it treats those "content differences as the major distinction among the disciplines" (Shanahan and Shanahan, p. 8). Disciplinary literacy goes much deeper by emphasizing the differences between the disciplines, and it teaches students the specific tools that experts in the field use, as well as their particular ways of reading and using text. For example, a content area literacy approach attempts to teach students reading strategies to learn or remember information from various texts, but the strategies themselves do not necessarily change; only the type of text that is being worked with changes depending upon the discipline.

A disciplinary literacy approach actually teaches students the differences that occur between disciplines, such as use of vocabulary. For example, the field of science uses words with Latin and Greek bases to classify things specifically, whereas the discipline of history uses phrases to "unify extensive collections of weakly interwoven groups and events (the *Gilded Age*) or to express a particular perspective on a particular event or action (*Dark Ages* versus *Middle Ages*)" (Shanahan and Shanahan, p. 10).

Whether teaching different reading strategies that can be used across the content areas, or teaching the actual differences between the types of texts and the thinking processes associated with texts for different disciplines, the list of useful resources that follows serves as a bridge for quick access to assist with planning and instruction.

TEACHER RESOURCES

Articles

Bull, K. B., and Dupuis, J. (2013). The role of young adult nonfiction in an interdisciplinary approach to teaching genetics. *ALAN Review, 41*(1), 33–45.
The authors show how English and biology teachers can use young adult (YA) nonfiction to teach genetics through the theory of evolution.

Gewertz, C. (2012). Districts gear up for shift to informational texts. *Education Digest, 78*(2), 10–14.
The author discusses the CCSS emphasis on nonfiction texts in English Language Arts (ELA) and examines efforts by teachers to comply with the standards by integrating autobiographies, historical documents, and scientific journals into curricula.

Gewertz, C. (2013). Teachers differ over meeting nonfiction rule. *Education Week, 31*(19), 1–15.
The article discusses ELA teachers' attitudes toward CCSS, which includes more nonfiction and informational texts and the effect of teaching classic literature.

Hirsch, E. D., Jr., and Hansel, L. (2013). Why content is king. *Educational Leadership, 71*(3), 28–33.
The article presents information on the focus on coherent curriculum, content knowledge, and reading comprehension by looking at text complexity, nonfiction and informational texts, and the CCSS.

Lesesne, T. S. (2013). Tell me a (real) story: The demand for literary nonfiction. *ALAN Review, 41*(1), 64–69.
The former president of Adolescents of NCTE (ALAN) provides a definition of literary nonfiction, its value, and how it differs from nonfiction in general.

Lopez, K. (2013). "That First Page": Some purposes and pleasures of teaching literary nonfiction. *California English, 19*(1), 23–25.
This classroom teacher details how the use of nonfiction has worked in allowing her students to internalize and communicate their experiences more effectively.

Newkirk, T. (2012). How we really comprehend nonfiction. *Educational Leadership*, *69*(6), 28–32.
This writing teacher suggests that students need to be taught how narratives work in nonfiction and how to incorporate narrative into their own writing. He addresses similarities between fictional and analytical writing.

Shanahan, T. (2013). You want me to read what? *Educational Leadership, 71*(3), 10–15.
The author looks at the CCSS, informational/explanatory writing, and student achievement in reading and discusses the balance of informational and fictional literature in US schools.

Shanahan, T., and Shanahan, C. (2012). What is disciplinary literacy and why does it matter? *Top Lang Disorders, 32*(1), 7–18.
This article explains the difference between content area literacy and disciplinary literacy.

Wineburg, S. (2013). Steering clear of the textbook. *Education Week, 33*(14), 2–3.
The author suggests the use of historical texts in ELA to satisfy the CCSS requirement for nonfiction.

Books

Alvermann, D. E., Gillis, V. R., and Phelps, S. F. (2012). *Content Area Reading and Literacy: Succeeding in Today's Diverse Classrooms* (7th ed.). Boston, MA: Pearson.
Providing classroom- and research-based teaching and learning strategies across the content areas, this textbook covers a wide range of topics including, but not limited to: literacy coaches collaborating with content teachers, politics associated with classroom materials and state and national agendas, and timely information about high-stakes testing.

Bean, T. W., Readence, J. E., and Baldwin, R. S. (2011). *Content Area Literacy: An Integrated Approach*. Dubuque, IA: Kendall/Hunt Publishing Company.
This textbook provides pre-service and in-service teachers with essential information and reference materials needed to develop effective lesson plans and strategies to promote learning across the content areas at the middle and secondary grade levels. Divided into two areas: (1) an introduction to content literacy and (2) strategies for teaching and learning across the content areas, this textbook also includes information about online reading assessments, online content inventories, and information related to the effective use of podcasts, blogging, and online research.

Bushman, J. H., and Haas, K. P. (2006). *Using Young Adult Literature in the English Classroom.* Upper Saddle River, NJ: Pearson.
This text discusses Young Adult Literature (YAL) and the classics, how to evaluate YAL, diversity and media in YAL, as well as using reader response and the reading-writing connection to teach it.

Cole, P. B. (2009). *Young Adult Literature in the 21st Century.* New York, NY: McGraw Hill.
This textbook covers trends in YAL, young adult readers themselves, and then is broken into chapters by genres, offering not only lists of young adult texts, but also teaching strategies to go along with them.

Conley, M. W. (2012). *Content Area Literacy: Learners in Context.* Boston, MA: Pearson Education Inc.
This book guides teachers by showing them how to promote learning in the content areas for today's students. Chapters discuss the diversity of students and how to plan lessons in alternate ways, how to use different types of texts in the classroom, how to activate prior knowledge, build vocabulary, increase motivation, develop writing skills, and how to guide students to better reading and critical literacy.

Fountas, I. C., and Pinnell, G. S. (2012). *Genre Study: Teaching with Fiction and Nonfiction Books.* Portsmouth, NH: Heinemann.
The authors advocate developing genre understandings so that students can apply their thinking to any genre. The focus is on inquiry-based learning with an emphasis on reading comprehension and the craft of writing.

Gura, M. (2014). *Teaching Literacy in the Digital Age: Inspiration for All Levels and Literacies.* New York, NY: International Society for Technology in Education.
This is an activity book tagged by level, technologies used, and literacy covered and all aligned with The International Society for Technology in Education (ISTE) and CCSS. Lessons can be easily adapted for special needs and English Language Learners (ELL) students.

McKenna, M. C., and Robinson, R. D. (2012). *Teaching through Text: Reading and Writing in the Content Areas* (2nd ed.). New York, NY: Longman.
This textbook provided readers with a comprehensive view of literacy in the content areas, including but not limited to understanding the importance of literacy in the content areas, a quick review of the literacy process, lesson planning, reading activities before and after reading, introducing and learning technical vocabulary, and multiple ways to extend learning through text.

Moore, D. W., and Moore, S. A. (2010). *Developing Readers and Writers in Content Areas K-12* (6th ed.). New York, NY: Longman.
This textbook is a practical tool for teachers in grades K–12. Opening with a compelling perspective on reasons for content area literacy instruction, the authors weave the reader through chapters about reading and writing processes, reading materials, learning independence, comprehension, vocabulary development, writing, and student research.

Nilsen, A. P., Blasingame, J., Nilsen, D., and Donelson, K. L. (2012). *Literature for Today's Young Adults.* Upper Saddle River, NJ: Pearson.
This is the latest edition of the classic YA text used in adolescent literature courses for many years.

Wadham, R. L., and Ostenson, J. W. (2013). *Integrating Young Adult Literature through the Common Core Standards.* Santa Barbara, CA: Libraries Unlimited.
This book offers teachers an introduction to YAL, an in-depth discussion of how YAL can work with the CCSS, and how teachers can evaluate a book's text complexity. It also discusses inquiry learning and walks one through the process of creating a unit plan by using an essential question or theme.

Vacca, R. T., Vacca, J. L., and Mraz, M. (2010). *Content Area Reading: Literacy and Learning across the Curriculum.* Boston, MA: Pearson.
This textbook offers teachers a broad perspective on content area reading and is divided into two major areas: learners, literacies, and texts; and instructional practices and strategies. With excellent chapters on new literacies and culturally responsive teaching as well as comprehensive chapters on building prior knowledge and guiding reading comprehension, teachers will find this an excellent resource to support their planning and instruction at a variety of grade levels.

Zygouris-Coe, V. (2015). *Teaching Discipline-specific Literacies in Grades 6-12: Preparing Students for College, Career, and Workforce Demands.* New York, NY: Routledge.
The author offers an approach to content-based literacy instruction that is aligned with CCSS but not specifically using YAL. A multitude of strategies is a useful feature.

Websites

http://www.adlit.org/adlit_101/improving_literacy_instruction_in_your_school/teaching_reading_and_writing_content_areas/
A helpful website for teachers to read about adolescent literature as well as suggestions for how to use it across a variety of content areas.

http://carnegie.org/fileadmin/Media/Publications/PDF/Content_Areas_report.pdf
A pdf containing a document from the Alliance for Excellent Education that discusses literacy instruction in the content areas.

https://lincs.ed.gov/publications/pdf/adolescent_literacy07.pdf
The National Institute for Literacy's document entitled "What Content Area Teachers Should Know about Content Area Literacy."

ADDITIONAL YA NONFICTION SELECTIONS

By Content Discipline

Arts

Chu, C., and Chang, L. (2012). *The Fashion Coloring Book*. New York, NY: HMH Books for Young Readers.
More than 50 famous designers are featured in this fashionable, fun text.

Kidd, C. (2013). *Go: A Kidd's Guide to Graphic Design*. New York, NY: Workman Publishing Company.
An interesting and fun look at graphic design that teaches about cropping, lines, and color. Ten projects are included for classroom application.

McMullan, J. (2014). *Leaving China: An Artist Paints his World War II Childhood*. Chapel Hill, NC: Algonquin Young Readers.
This artist tells his memoir by including some of his paintings that correlate to the parts of his life he is telling. This text also would work well in an ELA course.

Reef, C. (2014). *Frieda & Diego: Art, Love, Life*. London, UK: Clarion Books.
Reef explores the lives, accomplishments, and relationship of two famous Mexican artists.

Southgate, A., and Yishan, L. (2013). *Drawing Manga Women (Teen Guide to Drawing Manga)*. New York, NY: Rosen Central.
Southgate, A., and Yishan, L. (2012). *Drawing Manga Men (Teen Guide to Drawing Manga)*. New York, NY: Rosen Central.
These are two how-to books to teach the art of manga to teen artists.

English

Bolden, T. (2005). *Maritcha: A Nineteenth-century American Girl*. New York, NY: Harry N. Abrams.

This story is based on a memoir written by a black child born free in New York City during the days of slavery.

Hillenbrand, L. (2002). *Seabiscuit: An American Legend.* New York, NY: Ballantine Books.
A sportswriter tells the story of the unlikely rise to fame in thoroughbred racing.

Krakauer, J. (1999). *Into Thin Air: A Personal Account of the Mt. Everest Disaster.* New York: Anchor.
The book is a first-hand account of a catastrophic expedition up Mt. Everest written by the journalist and climber Krakauer.

Lewis, M. (2004). *Moneyball: The Art of Winning an Unfair Game.* New York, NY: W.W. Norton & Co.
The story of the quest for success in baseball following the career of Billy Beane was a page-turner before it was a film.

Yousafzai, M. (2013). *I Am Malala: The Girl Who Stood Up for Education and was Shot by the Taliban.* New York, NY: Little Brown & Co.
Reading Malawa's story told in her own voice provides a powerful lesson in any classroom.

Health

Burcaw, S. (2014). *Laughing at My Nightmare.* New York City: NY: Roaring Book Press.
This 2015 Young Adult Library Association (YALSA) nonfiction award finalist tells about the author's own experience with spinal muscular dystrophy.

Jarrow, G. (2014). *Red Madness: How a Medical Mystery Changed What We Eat.* Honesdale, PA: Calkins Creek.
This text tells the story about an outbreak of pellagra in the United States. The story discusses the disease, what scientists did about it, and how it changed the diet of Americans. This text also could be integrated into a science or health unit on diseases.

Kidder, T., and French, M. (2013). *Mountains beyond Mountains: The Quest of Dr. Paul Farmer, a Man Who Would Cure the World.* New York, NY: Delacorte Books for Young Readers.
An adapted biography of Dr. Paul Farmer, this story shares the heart-warming events of a man who spent his life trying to take modern medicine to Haiti.

Wagenen, M. V. (2014). *Popular: Vintage Wisdom for a Modern Geek.* Boston, MA: Dutton Books for Young Readers.
A YALSA 2015 nonfiction award finalist, this author tells her own story of how she used a 1950s teen etiquette book to become popular when she was in the 8th grade, including topics such as dieting, posture, and relating with peers.

Mathematics

Doxiadis, A., and Papadimitriou, H. (2009). *Logicomix: An Epic Search for Truth.* New York, NY: Bloomsbury.
This text is a graphic novel with nonfiction themes that tells Bertrand Russell's life story as he searches for the truth grappling with various mathematical concepts.

McKellar, D. (2009). *Kiss My Math: Showing Pre-algebra Who's Boss.* New York, NY: Plume.
McKellar, D. (2011). *Hot x: Algebra Exposed!* New York, NY: Plume.
McKellar, D. (2013). *Girls Get Curves: Geometry Takes Shape.* New York, NY: Plume.
McKellar's books all target girls and teach varying math concepts in humorous and relatable ways.

Science

Blum, D. (2011 Rpt.). *The Poisoner's Handbook: Murder and the Birth of Forensic Medicine in Jazz Age New York.* New York, NY: Penguin Books.
This book can provoke discussion in the science, history, or English classroom.

Fleischman, P. (2014). *Eyes Wide Open: Going Behind the Environmental Headlines.* Somerville, MA: Candlewick.
The author attempts to inform and inspire readers to understand the present environmental and sociological problems as well as possible solutions to improve them.

Kay, C. B., and Cousteau, P. (2010). *Going Blue: A Teen Guide to Saving Our Oceans, Lakes, Rivers, & Wetlands.* Minneapolis, MN: Free Spirit Publishing.
Using the concept of service learning, this book instructs teens about the current plight of our earth's water supplies and environmentally appropriate actions that students can implement in everyday life to help preserve our remaining resources.

Kean, S. (2011). *The Disappearing Spoon: And Other True Tales of Madness, Love, and the History of the World from the Periodic Table of the Elements.* New York, NY: Back Bay Books.

Kean, S. (2013). *The Violinist's Thumb: And Other Lost Tales of Love, War, and Genius as Written by Our Genetic Code.* New York, NY: Back Bay Books.

Kean, S. (2014). *The Tale of the Dueling Neurosurgeons: The History of the Human Brain as Revealed by True Stories of Trauma, Madness, and Recovery.* New York, NY: Little, Brown, & Company.

Kean educates readers about a facet of science in each book using witty prose and funny anecdotes.

Keller, M. (2009). *Charles Darwin's* On the Origin of the Species: *A Graphic Adaptation.* Emmaus, PA: Rodale Books.

A graphic informational text based *On the Origin of the Species*, this text provides readers with beautiful illustrations.

Ottaviani, J. (2013). *Primates: The Fearless Science of Jane Goodall, Dian Fossey, and Biruté Galdikas.* New York, NY: First Second.

A graphic nonfiction narrative, this text tells the stories of three female scientists who studied chimpanzees, gorillas, and orangutans.

Social Studies

Bascomb, N. (2013). *The Nazi Hunters: How a Team of Spies and Survivors Hunted and Captured the World's Most Notorious Nazi.* New York, NY: Arthur A. Levine.

This book tells the story about the search and capture of Adolf Eichmann and includes historic pictures and documents.

Farrell, M. C. (2014). *Pure Grit: How American World War II Nurses Survived Battle and Prison Camp in the Pacific.* New York, NY: Abrams Books for Young Readers.

Based on stories of nurses during World War II who were stationed in the Philippines, this text shares how US nurses were caught and imprisoned by the Japanese.

Fleming, C. (2014). *The Family Romanov: Murder, Rebellion and the Fall of Imperial Russia.* New York, NY: Shwartz & Wade.

This text is a biography of the Romanov family told through the use of pictures, letters, and diary entries.

Hopkinson, D. (2012). *Titanic: Voices from the Disaster.* New York, NY: Scholastic.

This text shares the stories about passengers and crew of the famous cruise ship, the Titanic.

McCully, E. A. (2014). *Ida M. Tarbell: The Woman Who Challenged Big Business—And Won!* New York, NY: Clarion Books.

This text is a biography of Ida Tarbell who became the head of Standard Oil and Trust at a time in history when it was unheard of for a woman to serve as the CEO of a company.

Mitchell, D. (2014). *The Freedom Summer Murders.* New York, NY: Scholastic Press.

This text narrates the story of the freedom summer murders including the disappearance of three freedom summer workers, the search for their bodies, and the attempt to prosecute guilty parties. Pictures from the time period help the reader to visualize the story and make its story line about social justice more tangible.

Sheinkin, S. (2012). *Bomb: The Race to Build—and Steal—the World's Most Dangerous Weapon.* Flashpoint.

This story explains how the atomic bomb was invented, and narrates the events that surround its creation.

Sheinkin, S. (2014). *The Port Chicago 50: Disaster, Mutiny, and the Fight for Civil Rights.* New York, NY: Roaring Book Press.

This book tells the story of 50 black navy sailors who refused to continue to load bombs after 320 servicemen, many whom were friends and family, were killed in an explosion at Port Chicago during World War II.

Walker, S. M. (2014). *Boundaries: How the Mason-Dixon Line Settled a Family Feud and Divided a Nation.* Somerville, MA: Candlewick.

The author tells the story of the Mason-Dixon Line by using maps, period pictures, and documents, and explains how the line was actually drawn.

Index

About the Contributors

Jacqueline Bach, a former high school teacher, is the Elena and Albert LeBlanc associate professor of English Education at Louisiana State University and former coeditor of *The ALAN Review*, a journal dedicated to the study and teaching of young adult literature (YAL). Her scholarship examines how YAL engages educators and students in conversations about social issues, the ways in which popular culture informs pedagogy, and the preparation of secondary English language arts teachers. She has published articles in *The English Journal*, *Changing English*, *Signal*, and *Voices from the Middle*.

Steven T. Bickmore is an associate professor of English education at Louisiana State University. He has served as an editor of *The ALAN Review* (2009–2014). He is also one of the founders and coeditors of *Study and Scrutiny: Research in Young Adult Literature*. His research interests include the induction and mentoring of novice teachers and the demonstration of how pre-service and novice English teachers negotiate the teaching of literature using YAL, especially around the issues of race, class, and gender (sbick@ lsu.edu).

Paul E. Binford served as a middle and high school public school teacher and administrator and is currently an assistant professor of Secondary Social Studies Teacher Education at Louisiana State University. He has published two state history teacher wraparound editions, *Louisiana: Our History, Our Home* and *A Place Called Mississippi* as well as *Lincoln's Cabinet and the Sumter Crisis*—a historical classroom simulation. His scholarly work has appeared in a variety of journals, including *Theory and Research in Social Education*, the *International Journal of Social Education*, *American*

Educational History Journal, Sound Historian, Louisiana English Journal, and the *ALAN Review.*

Kelly Byrne Bull is associate professor at Notre Dame of Maryland University where she teaches courses in language and culture, literacy, literature, and educational research. She is chair of CEE's Commission on the Study and Teaching of Adolescent Literature and has published many journal articles, book chapters, and curricular resources for teachers. Visit her current project, World Literature for Young Adults: A Multimedia Project at http://ya-worldlit.blogspot.com/p/main-page.html.

Karina R. Clemmons is an associate professor of Secondary Education at the University of Arkansas at Little Rock. Dr. Clemmons has taught English language arts in English for Speaker of Other Languages classrooms in middle school, high school, and abroad. She researches, publishes, and presents in the areas of YAL, teacher education, technology in education, and content literacy.

James M. Fetterly, PhD, has taught secondary mathematics in public schools for five years and coached middle school mathematics teachers for an additional two years. His professional interests are related to mathematical creativity and problem posing. In 2007, he began training teacher candidates in the art of knowing and learning mathematics at Florida State University. For another four years he continued to work with pre- and in-service teachers at the University of Arkansas at Little Rock. Now Dr. Fetterly is an assistant professor in the Department of Mathematics at the University of Central Arkansas.

Susan L. Groenke earned a BA in English in 1993 and an MA in Curriculum & Instruction in 1995 from Virginia Tech in Blacksburg, Virginia. She then taught English language arts at the middle and high school levels for six years before returning to Virginia Tech to pursue her doctoral degree in Curriculum & Instruction. In 1999, Groenke was nationally board certified in English Language Arts for Adolescents. She received her PhD in 2003. Her research interests include adolescent motivation to read and adolescent understandings of YAL. Groenke is currently the program advisor for the English education program at the University of Tennessee in Knoxville. She teaches courses in secondary English methods, composition pedagogy, and YAL. Groenke is former editor of *English Leadership Quarterly*, an NCTE publication, and in 2014 became the director of the Center for Children's and YAL on the UTK campus.

Judith A. Hayn taught 15 years in public schools and is currently a professor of English education at the University of Arkansas at Little Rock. Her research focuses on social justice issues in YAL; she has published numerous reviews, articles, and teacher curriculum materials. She coedited the 2012 text, *Teaching Young Adult Literature Today: Insights, Consideration, and Perspectives for the Classroom Teacher*, also published by Rowman & Littlefield.

Melanie Kittrell Hundley taught middle and high school in Georgia for many years and is currently an assistant professor at Vanderbilt University. Her research focuses on digital, multimodal, and transmedia storytelling in YAL. She has published numerous book chapters, book reviews, articles, and instructional materials. She is the past coeditor of *The ALAN Review*, the leading journal for YAL.

Jeffrey S. Kaplan, PhD is an associate professor at the School of Teaching, Learning and Leadership, College of Education, University of Central Florida, Orlando. He is the former president of ALAN (2012–2013), Assembly on Literature for Adolescents and research connections editor for *The ALAN* Review. He is the current president of the National Council Teachers of English Standing Committee Against Censorship (2015–2017). He coedited with Judith Hayn, PhD, *Teaching Young Adult Literature Today: Insights, Considerations and Perspectives for the Classroom Teacher* (Rowman and Littlefield, 2012). Educator, author and consultant, Jeffrey Kaplan is the author of many refereed publications on teaching strategies and methodologies for improving classroom instruction using literacy material geared for adolescent readers.

Kent Layton is currently an associate professor of reading education at the University of Arkansas at Little Rock where he teaches primarily in the graduate programs. He has authored book chapters and articles in the areas of text complexity issues, associated diagnostic assessments, technology and literacy, leadership of distance learning, content area reading, cloze procedure, and alternative certification pathways. In addition to his teaching, he has served as an education dean at the College of Coastal Georgia, the University of West Georgia, and Arkansas State University.

Amanda L. Nolen is the interim chair of the Psychology Department at the University of Arkansas at Little Rock. She was an associate professor of educational psychology prior to that position. She is the former chief operating officer for the Holmes Partnership, a national educational reform consortium. Nolen has published widely on topics such as emerging research methods, educational psychology, and teacher education reform.

Heather A. Olvey is a former graduate research assistant in the School of Education of the University of Arkansas at Little Rock, and teaches high school English in the Pulaski County School District in Arkansas. She has presented her research in YAL at the International Reading Association conference and has made contributions to several professional publications.

Robert Prickett, PhD, is an associate professor of English education and acting department of English chairperson at Winthrop University. Prickett has taught courses in secondary methods, educational technology, and adolescent literature. With a specialized focus on English education, his most recent contributions to the field are bringing together areas of personal and professional interest: popular culture, media and technology, YAL, and teaching.

Rachel L. Wadham is currently the Education and Juvenile Collections librarian at Brigham Young University where she also teaches courses in children's and adolescent literature. Her research focuses on literacy and the Common Core as well as curriculum integration; she has published numerous reviews, articles, and books. Her books *Integrating Young Adult Literature Though the Common Core* and *Integrating Children's Literature Though the Common Core State Standards* are published by ABC-CLIO.

Trena L. Wilkerson taught in public high schools for 18 years and has been in teacher education for over 20 years. Currently, she is a professor of mathematics education at Baylor University in Waco, Texas. Her research and curriculum work focus on lesson study, student learning, teacher development, and the use of literature in problem solving. She has made over 200 presentations at state, national, and international conferences; and published journal articles, book chapters, and curriculum material. She codirected a 15-year initiative addressing young adult learners in mathematics.

Betty K. Wood spent over 20 years in the public schools teaching secondary mathematics and gifted education. She is currently a professor of middle childhood education at the University of Arkansas at Little Rock. Her research focuses on mathematics education and specifically on infusing creativity into mathematics teaching and learning. Dr. Wood has presented her ideas in national and state conferences and publications.